Other books by Oswald J. Smith

David Brainerd, Man of Prayer
The Marvels of Grace
Tales of the Mission Field
The Adventures of Andy McGinnis
Poems of a Lifetime

Other books in the Oswald J. Smith Treasury:

The Salvation of God
The Challenge of Missions
The Enduement of Power
The Man God Uses
The Story of My Life
Is the Antichrist At Hand?

The Peoples Church, Toronto
374 Sheppard Avenue East
Willowdale, Ontario
M2N 3B6   Canada

© Oswald J. Smith 1959
This edition published by Bible Faith Church, Toronto, Canada
2006 with permission
ISBN 0-9781188-0-4

THE PASSION FOR SOULS

by

OSWALD J. SMITH, LITT.D.

Founder of The Peoples Church, Toronto

Foreword by

DR. GAETANO SICILIA

DR. BILLY GRAHAM

HARMONY PRINTING LIMITED
TORONTO, CANADA

3

·

FOREWORD
by
Dr. Gaetano Sicilia

In the summer of 1998, I came across Dr. O.J. Smith's book entitled "The Passion for Souls". I quickly became absorbed in the plea that Dr. Smith makes to each and every Christian in this small, power-packed book.

As a pastor of a growing congregation, I am particularly touched by his words; "the kind of evangelism we need is that evangelism that will hold up the hands of the pastor and in every possible way support and encourage him." (Chapter 11)

I went on to read most of the available works by Dr. Smith. I found myself consistently referencing and giving away copies of "The Passion for Souls" to visiting itinerants in our church. I finally decided that I wanted to purchase enough copies to sow into the foreign field, which God was allowing us to visit for Kingdom purposes. I soon discovered, to my amazement, that the book was out of print.

I sensed strongly to undertake efforts to have the book reprinted and so I am extremely thankful for the wonderful Christians at Operation Mobilisation in the U.K. for allowing this Canadian 21st century reprinting of a missionary "classic" that should be added to the library of any man or woman that truly wants to complete the Great Commission outlined in St. Mark 16:15-18.

It is my heart-felt prayer that, this reprinting of the 1980's copy of the "The Passion for Souls", will stir a new generation of committed men and women of God to go and fulfill the great mission of Christ Jesus with that "passion for souls" that Dr. Smith so clearly articulates in this wonderful book.

In The Master's Service
Dr. Gaetano Sicilia
www.biblefaith.com
July 2006
Toronto, Canada

5

FOREWORD
by
Dr. Billy Graham

The heart and core of Youth for Christ is the missionary burden and vision. Thousands of people on foreign soil are finding Christ through this organization. The missionary vision that transformed Youth for Christ several years ago was largely the product of the vision, counsel, advice, leadership and comradeship of Dr. Oswald J. Smith.

As a Missionary Statesman he has no peer. Around the world the name Oswald J. Smith symbolizes world-wide evangelization. His preaching tours, the tremendous amounts of money raised and his God-given vision have been the dynamic encouragement and drive of countless missionary societies. When the missionary vision had dimmed a few years ago, a voice from Toronto kept crying in the wilderness: "Missions! Missions! Missions!" and evangelical Christians across the American continent began to awake once again to their responsibility to the heathen. His challenging addresses have been used of God to help raise millions of dollars for missions. As a *missionary* he exemplifies a passion for souls.

As an Evangelist, he has a burning passion for the souls of men. His intense drive, his powerful, clear and concise presentation of the Gospel, his God-given ability to give an invitation have proved on hundreds of platforms and at a hundred altars that he has been generously endowed with the gift of evangelism. His campaigns in Australia, Ireland, Jamaica, and South Africa will never be forgotten. In South America, where he preached to audiences of 25,000 people with many turned away, there were 4,500 first-time decisions for Christ. I met ministers whose lives and work have been transformed. Certainly the Lord used him in a unique and tremendous way to stir the hearts of Christians as they have not been touched perhaps in the history of the Evangelical Movement. As an *evangelist* he exemplifies a passion for souls.

As a Pastor the great ministry of The Peoples Church proclaims to all the world that this man has learned the secret of a successful pastor

– the heart and core of the great Peoples Church in Toronto is evangelism and missions. Few other pastors have had so long and fruitful a pastorate as that of Oswald J. Smith. I have spoken in the Peoples Church on several occasions and on every occasion I have been amazed to find it packed and jammed to capacity. Only Heaven's records know how many souls have knelt at the Peoples Church altar and found Christ. As a *pastor* he exemplifies a passion for souls.

As an Author his books and pamphlets have been translated into scores of languages. It is impossible for one to read a page in any of his many books and not catch something of the intensity with which he loves the souls of men. The pen loses none of its enthusiasm, power and burning challenge. His books have been used by the Holy Spirit to sear into the very depths of my own soul and have had a tremendous influence of my personal life and ministry. As an *author* he exemplifies a passion for souls.

As a Poet and Hymn-writer his songs are loved and sung around the world. Who can listen to that great hymn, "Then Jesus Came," or to "God Understands." "The Glory of His Presence," or "The Song of the Soul Set Free," without feeling the passion of this man for the souls of men? In scores of meetings I have seen the hearts of people melted and broken by the singing of these songs. His best-know hymn, "Saved," has been a testimony to multitudes. As a *hymn-writer* he exemplifies a passion for souls.

As a man his utter consecration and devotion to the cause of our Lord Jesus Christ and the advancement of His Kingdom have given new hope, courage and inspiration to thousands of young preachers. His devoted prayer life and his Spirit-filled personal life have been a blessing to thousands. No one can be in his presence for five minutes without seeing the flame of his soul. As a *man* he exemplifies a passion for souls.

It seems that only once in a generation does God raise up a man with so many talents and gifts. The driving passion of this man's life will live throughout generations to come, should Christ tarry. Certainly no man in our day is more qualified to write on a passion for souls. As this book goes forth, it is our earnest prayer that others, too, might catch this burden vision and flaming passion.

INTRODUCTION
By Rev. JONATHAN GOFORTH, D.D.

DR. SMITH'S book, "The Passion for Souls", for its size is the most powerful plea for Revival I have ever read. He has truly been led by the Spirit of God in preparing it. To his emphasis for the need of a Holy Spirit Revival I can give the heartiest amen. What I saw of Revival in Korea and in China is in fullest accord with the Revival called for in this book.

It is most timely that Dr. Smith has called attention to man effort and man method in modern Revival. If we all had faith to wait upon God in intense believing prayer there would be genuine Holy Ghost Revival, and the living God would get all the glory. In Manchuria and China, when we did nothing else than give the address and let the people pray, and kept out of sight as far as possible, we saw the mightiest manifestations of Divine power.

Had I the wealth of a millionaire I would put "The Passion for Souls" in every Christian home on this continent and confidently look for a Revival which would sweep round the world.

Toronto, Canada   J.G.

NOTE: *Written for the first seven chapters.*

CONTENTS

CHAPTER I

THE OUTPOURING OF THE SPIRIT

IT was 1904. Wales was aflame. The nation had drifted far from God. The spiritual conditions were low indeed. Church attendance was poor. And sin abounded on every side.

Suddenly, like an unexpected tornado, the Spirit of God swept over the land. The churches were crowded so that multitudes were unable to get in. Meetings lasted from ten in the morning until twelve at night. Three definite services were held each day. Evan Roberts was the human instrument, but there was very little preaching. Singing, testimony, and prayer were the chief features. There were no hymn books; they had learnt the hymns in childhood. No choir, for everybody sang. No collection; and no advertising.

Nothing had ever come over Wales with such far-reaching results. Infidels were converted, drunkards, thieves, and gamblers saved; and thousands reclaimed to respectability. Confessions of awful sins were heard on every side. Old debts were paid. The theatre had to leave for want of patronage. Mules in the coal mines refused to work, being unused to kindness. In five weeks 20,000 joined the churches.

In the year 1835 Titus Coan landed on the shore belt of Hawaii. On his first tour multitudes flocked to hear him. They thronged him so that he had scarcely time to eat. Once he preached three times before he had a chance to take breakfast. He felt that God was strangely at work.

In 1837 the slumbering fires broke out. Nearly the whole population became an audience. He was ministering to 15,000 people. Unable to reach them, they came to him, and settled down to a two years' camp meeting. There was not an hour, day or night, when an audience of 2,000 to 6,000 would not rally to the signal of the bell.

There was trembling, weeping, sobbing, and loud crying for mercy, sometimes too loud for the preacher to be heard: and in hundreds of cases his hearers fell in a swoon. Some would cry out, "The two-edged sword is cutting me to pieces." The wicked scoffer who came to make sport dropped like a dog, and cried, "God has struck me!" Once while preaching in the open field to 2,000 people, a man cried out, "What must I do to be saved?" and prayed the publican's prayer, and the entire congregation took up the cry for mercy. For half an hour Mr. Coan could get no chance to speak, but had to stand still and see God work.

Quarrels were made up, drunkards reclaimed, adulterers converted, and murderers revealed and pardoned. Thieves returned stolen property, and sins of a lifetime were renounced. In one year 5,244 joined the Church. There were 1,705 baptized on one Sunday, and 2,400 sat down at the Lord's table, once sinners of the blackest type, now saints of God. When Mr. Coan left he had himself received and baptized 11,960 persons.

In the little town of Adams, across the line, in the year 1821, a young lawyer made his way to a secluded spot in the woods to pray. God met him there and he was wondrously converted, and soon after filled with the Holy Spirit. That man was Chas. G. Finney.

The people heard about it, became deeply interested, and as though by common consent, gathered into the meeting house in the evening. Mr. Finney was present. The Spirit of God came on them in mighty, convicting power, and a Revival started. It then spread to the surrounding country, until finally nearly the whole of the Eastern States was held in the grip of a mighty Awakening. Whenever Mr. Finney preached the Spirit was poured out. Frequently God went before him so that when he arrived at the place he found the people already crying out for mercy.

Sometimes the conviction of sin was so great and caused such fearful wails of anguish that he had to stop preaching until it subsided. Ministers and church members were converted. Sinners were reclaimed by thousands. And for years the mighty work of grace went on. Men had never witnessed the like in their lives before.

• • • • •

I have recalled to your minds three historical incidents of the Outpouring of the Holy Spirit. Hundreds of others might be cited. But these are sufficient to show what I mean. And this is what we need to-day more than anything else. When I remember that such an

Outpouring has come to China, India, Korea, Africa, England, Wales, the States, the Islands of the Seas, and many other places but that Canada, our Dominion, our own beloved country, has never in its history experienced a national Revival, my heart cries out to God for such a Manifestation of Himself.

Do we need it? Listen! How many of our churches are more than half empty Sunday after Sunday? What a multitude there are who never enter God's house? How many mid-week prayer meetings are alive and prosperous? Where is the hunger for spiritual things?

And Missions – the lands beyond the seas, heathen darkness – what are we doing? Does the fact that multitudes are perishing ever cause us an anxious thought? Have we grown selfish?

What about the tremendous wealth that God has given us? Take the Unites States as an example, the richest nation in the world to-day, and the major portion of her wealth in the hands of professing Christians. And yet the United States spent more on gum in one year than she spent on Missions. How many Christians are giving God even the tenth of what He gives them?

Then take our colleges and seminaries, both at home and on the mission field where higher criticism is taught. We are told that Jesus never performed any miracles, never rose from the dead, was not born of a virgin, did not die as our Substitute, and is not coming again.

How many professing Christians are living the Christ-life before men? Oh, how like the world we are becoming! How little opposition do we find! Where are the persecutions that were heaped on the Early Church? How easy it is now to be a Christian!

And what of the Ministry? Does the minister grip, convert, and save by his message? How many souls are won through the preaching of the Word? Oh, my friends, we are loaded down with countless church activities, while the real work of the Church, that of evangelizing the world and winning the lost, is almost entirely neglected.

Where is the conviction of sin we used to know? Is it a thing of the past? Let us look at one of Finney's meetings. Oh that we could repeat it to-day. He tells us that one time when he was conducting meetings in Antwerp, an old man invited him to preach in a small school house near by. When he arrived the place was packed so that he could barely find standing room near the door. He spoke for a long time. At last he began to press home upon them the fact that they were an ungodly community; for they held no services in their district. All at once they were stricken with conviction. The Spirit of God came like a thunderbolt upon them. One by one they fell on their knees, or prostrate on the floor, crying for mercy. In two minutes they were all down, and Mr. Finney had to stop preaching for he was unable to make himself heard. At last he got the attention of the old man who was sitting in the middle of the room and gazing around him in utter amazement, he shouted to him at the top of his voice to pray. Then taking them one by one he pointed them to Jesus. The old man took charge of the meeting while he went to another. All night it continued, so deep was the conviction of sin. The results were permanent, and one of the young converts became a most successful minister of the Gospel.

Ah, yes, men have forgotten God. Sin flourishes on every side. And the pulpit fails to grip. And I know of nothing less than the Outpouring of God's Spirit that can meet the situation. Such a Revival has transformed scores and hundreds of communities, and it can transform ours.

Now, how may we secure such an Outpouring of the Spirit? You answer, by prayer. True, but there is something before prayer. We will have to deal first of all with the question of sin; for unless our lives are right in the sight of God, unless sin has been put away, we may pray until doomsday, and the Revival will never come. "Your iniquities have separated between you and your God, and your sins have hid His face from you so that He will not hear." (Isaiah 59:2)

Probably our best guide here is the prophecy of Joel. Let us look at it. It is a call to repentance. God is anxious to bless His people, but sin has withheld the blessing. And, so, in His love and compassion He brings a fearful judgment upon them. We have it described in chapters one and two. It has almost reached the gates of the city. But see – how great is His love! Notice verses twelve to fourteen of chapter two, where He says, "Turn ye even to Me with all your heart, and with fasting, and with weeping, and with mourning; and rend your heart, and not your garments, and turn unto the Lord your God; for He is gracious and merciful, slow to anger, and of great kindness, and repenteth Him of the evil. Who knoweth if He will return and repent, and leave a blessing behind Him?"

Now my friend, I don't know what your sin is. You know and God knows. But I want you to think about it, for you may as well stop praying and rise from your knees until you have dealt with it, and put it away. "If I regard iniquity in my heart, the Lord will not hear me." Let God search your heart and reveal the hindrance. Sin must be confessed and put away.

It may be you will have to forsake some cherished idol. It may be you will have to make restitution. Perhaps you are withholding from God, robbing Him of His own. But this is your affair, not mine. It lies between you and God.

Now notice verses fifteen to seventeen. The prophet has called for a prayer meeting. Sin has been confessed and forsaken. Now they may pray. And they are to entreat God for His own name's sake, lest the nations say, "Where is their God?" They are dead in earnest now and their prayer is going to prevail. Listen! "Blow the trumpet in Zion, sanctify a fast, call a solemn assembly: gather the people, sanctify the congregation; assemble the elders, gather the children. Let the priests, the ministers of the Lord, weep between the porch and the altar, and let them say, 'Spare Thy people, O Lord, and give not Thine heritage to reproach, that the heathen should rule over them: wherefore should they say among the people, "Where is their God?"'"

Ah! my brethren, are you praying? Do you plead with God for this city? Are you beseeching Him night and day for an Outpouring of His Spirit? For now is the hour to pray. We are told of a time in the work of Finney, when the Revival had died out. He then made a covenant with the young people to pray at sunrise, noon and sunset in their closets for one week. The Spirit was poured out again, and before the week ended the meetings were thronged.

And, of course, it must be believing prayer, prayer that expects. If God stirs up hearts to pray for a Revival it is a sure sign that He wants to send one, and He is always true to His Word. "There shall be showers of blessing." His promises never fail. Have we faith? Do we expect an Awakening?

Now notice the speedy answer in verse eighteen. "Then!" After they had forsaken sin and cried unto God in prayer. "Then will the Lord be jealous for His land, and pity His people." The answer is not long in coming once the conditions have been met.

Oh, my brethren, the trouble is not with God. It lies right here with ourselves. He is willing, more than willing. But we are not ready. And He is waiting for us. Are we going to keep Him waiting long?

CHAPTER II

THE RESPONSIBILITY FOR REVIVAL

AS far back as I can remember my heart has burned within me whenever I have heard or read accounts of the mighty work of God in the great Revivals of past years. The heroic missionaries of the Cross in foreign lands, and the lonely men of God in the home field around whom these gracious Visitations have centered, have always been a source of untold inspiration to my life. David Brainerd, Adoniram Judson, Chas. G. Finney, Robt. Murray McCheyne – these and many others have been my bosom companions and friends.

I have watched them, listened to them, lived with them, until I have almost felt the spirit of the atmosphere in which they moved. Their trials and hardships, their prayers and tears; their joys and sorrows, their glorious triumphs and victorious achievements have thrilled my very soul, and I have fallen down upon my face and exclaimed with the prophet of old: "Oh, that Thou wouldst rend the heavens, and that Thou wouldst come down!"

The great Awakening of the eighteenth century under John Wesley, the stirring Irish Manifestation of 1859, the glorious American Visitation in the nineteenth century under Chas. G. Finney, and in our own day the mighty Welsh Revival of 1904-05 – Manifestations such as these have been my meat and drink for years past. I have heard again the uncontrollable sob and groan of the convicted, the exceeding bitter cry of the penitent, and the unspeakable expressions of joy of the delivered. And I have sighed within myself for another such Manifestation of God's presence and power.

From my boyhood it has been my delight to read more or less of God's work along these lines, but lately I have been led to lay all else aside and to literally devour everything I could lay hands on regarding Revival work. And as I studied the lives of those whom God has signally used all down the centuries, especially the labours of the Puritans, the early Methodists, and others of later years, and saw how wonderfully they were owned of Him – how they worked for, expected and got what they sought – I was compelled to admit that I could see nothing like it to-day either in my own ministry or in the

19

ministry of others. The average church does not aim at, let alone get, results. Men preach and never even dream of anything happening. Oh, how far away we have drifted! How powerless we have become!

It is reported that there were 7,000 churches that did not win a single soul for Jesus Christ in an entire year. That means that 7,000 ministers preached the Gospel for a whole year without reaching even one lost soul. Supposing that they preached, putting it at a low average, on forty Sundays, not including extra meetings, that would mean that these 7,000 ministers preached 560,000 sermons in a single year. Think of the work, the labour, the money expended in salaries, etc., to make this possible. And yet 560,000 sermons preached by 7,000 ministers in 7,000 churches to tens of thousands of hearers during a period of twelve months, failed to bring a single soul to Christ.

Now, my brethren, there is something radically wrong somewhere. There is either something the matter with these 7,000 ministers or else with their 560,000 sermons, or both.

In reading over the Twelve Rules of the early Methodist church I was struck with the fact that they aimed at and looked upon soul-winning as their supreme task. Let me quote from one of them: "You have nothing to do but to save souls. Therefore spend and be spent in this work. It is not your business to preach so many times; but to save as many souls as you can; to bring as many sinners as you possibly can to repentance, and with all your power to build them up in that holiness, without which they cannot see the Lord." – From "The Twelve Rules." – John Wesley.

The practical application of this rule is demonstrated in the life of Wm. Bramwell, one of their most remarkable men. "He was not, as the words are commonly understood, a great preacher. But if that man is the best physician who performs the most cures, that is the best preacher who is the instrument of bringing the greatest number of souls to God; and in this view Mr. Bramwell will be entitled to rank amongst the greatest and best Christian ministers." – Memoir of Wm. Bramwell.

John Oxtoby was so used of God that he was able to say: "I am witnessing daily the conversion of sinners, I seldom go out but God gives me some Fruit."

It was said of John Smith, one of their most wonderfully anointed men and the spiritual father of thousands, that "he ceased to estimate all Preaching, and indeed all ministerial labour except as it produced saving effects. 'I am determined by the grace of God to aim at souls,' he exclaimed. 'A minister of the Gospel is sent to turn men from darkness to light, and from the power of Satan to God!' Of that species of preaching which only produced intellectual pleasure, he had a holy abhorrence. Nothing can be more characteristic of the man than his remark to a friend, on sermons in which power of intellect or imagination is almost exclusively predominant: 'They achieve nothing, sir.' " – Life of John Smith.

"I cannot tell how they get their time over, who drag on and see no Fruit. Were that so in my case I should be ready to conclude that I was out of my place." – Thos. Taylor.

"If your hearts be not set on the end of your labors, and you do not long to see the conversion and edification of your hearers, and do not study and preach in hope, you are not likely to see much fruit of it. It is an ill sign of a false, self-seeking heart, that can be content to be still doing, and see no fruit of their labour." – Richard Baxter.

Then I compared the results of my ministry with the promises of God. In Jer. 23:29, I read: "Is not My Word like a Fire, saith the Lord; and like a Hammer that breaketh the rock in pieces?" And in Eph. 6:17, "The Sword of the Spirit, which is the Word of God." But the more I pondered over it, the more I was convinced that in my ministry the Word of God was not a Fire, a Hammer, and a Sword. It did not burn, break and pierce. There was no execution. Heb. 4:12 declares that "the Word of God is quick and powerful, and sharper than any two-edged sword, piercing even to the dividing asunder of soul and spirit, and of the joints and marrow, and is a discerner of the thoughts and intents of the heart." I had never seen it so. John Wesley saw it. John Smith was a constant observer of it. David Brainerd witnessed its sharpness; but I did not. "So shall My Word be that goeth forth out of my mouth; it shall not return to me void, but

21

it shall accomplish that which I please, and it shall prosper in the thing whereto I sent it." (Isa. 55:11.) And I knew that this wonderful promise had not been fulfilled in my preaching. I had no evidence such as Paul, Wm. Bramwell and Chas. G. Finney that it did not return void many and many a time. And I had a right to the evidence. Was it any wonder that I began to challenge my preaching?

And not only my preaching, but my prayer life as well. This also had to be challenged and tested by the Outcome. And I was forced to admit that the confident assertion of Jer. 33:3, "Call unto Me, and I will answer thee, and show thee great and mighty things, which thou knowest not," was not realized in my experience. The "great and mighty things" were almost daily witnessed by Evan Roberts, Jonathan Goforth and others, but not by me. My prayers were not definitely and daily answered. Hence, John 14:13-14, "Whatsoever ye shall ask in My name, that will I do," and "If ye shall ask anything in My Name, I will do it," was not real in my case. To me these promises where not vital since I asked for many things that I did not receive, and this was not according to the promise.

Thus I came to realize that there was something radically wrong with my prayer-life. And in reading the autobiography of Chas. G. Finney, I found that he, too, had experienced the same failure. "I was particularly struck," he relates, "the fact that the prayers that I had listened to, from week to week, were not, that I could see, answered. Indeed, I understood from their utterances in prayer, and from other remarks in their meetings, that those who offered them did not regard them as answered.

They exhorted each other to wake up and be engaged, and to pray earnestly for a Revival, asserting that if they did their duty, prayed for the Outpouring of the Spirit, and were in earnest, that the Spirit of God would be poured out, that they would have a Revival, and that the impenitent would be converted. But in their prayers and conference meetings they would continually confess, substantially that they were making no progress in securing a Revival.

This inconsistency, the fact that they prayed so much and were not answered, was a sad stumbling-block to me. I knew not what to make of it. It was a question in my mind whether I was to understand that these persons were not truly Christians, and therefore did not prevail with God; or did I misunderstand the promises and teachings of the Bible on this subject, or was I to conclude that the Bible was not true? Here was something inexplicable to me, and it seemed, at one time, that it would almost drive me into skepticism. It seemed to me that the teachings of the Bible did not at all accord with the facts which were before my eyes.

On one occasion, when I was in the prayer meeting, I was asked if I did not desire that they should pray for me. I told them no, because I did not see that God answered their prayers. I said, 'I suppose I need to be prayed for, for I am conscious that I am a sinner; but I do not see that it will do any good for you to pray for me; for you are continually asking, but you do not receive. You have been praying for a Revival ever since I have been in Adams, and yet you have it not' ".

When John Wesley concluded his message he cried to God to "confirm His Word," to "set to His Seal," and to "bear witness to His Word." And God did. Sinners were stricken immediately, and began to cry for mercy under fearful conviction of sin, and soon after, in a moment they were set at liberty, and filled with unspeakable joy in the knowledge of a present Salvation. In his wonderful Journal he sets down what his eyes witnessed, and his ears heard in the following words:

"We understood that many were offended at the cries of those on whom the power of God came; and among whom was a physician, who was much afraid there might be fraud or imposture in the case. To-day one whom he had known many years was the first who broke out in strong cries and tears. He could hardly believe his own eyes and ears. He went and stood close to her, and observed every symptom, till great drops of sweat ran down her face, and all her bones shook. He then knew not what to think, being clearly convinced it was not fraud, nor yet any natural disorder. But when both her soul and body were healed in a moment, he acknowledged the finger of God."

Such was also the experience of the early Church. "Now when they heard this they were pricked in their hearts, and said unto Peter and to the rest of the apostles, Men and brethren, what shall we do?"

(Acts 2:37) "Long time therefore abode they speaking boldly in the name of the Lord, which gave testimony unto the Word of His grace, and granted signs and wonders to be done by their hands." (Acts 14:3.) They prayed "that signs and wonders" might "be done." (Acts 4:30.) And Paul declared that the Gospel is "the power of God unto Salvation." (Rom. 1:16.) Yet all this was utterly foreign to my work.

In the Irish Revival of 1859, "signs and wonders" were seen on every side. Among the early Methodists they were of daily occurrence. But with me the Gospel was not "the power of God unto Salvation." God did not "confirm His Word," "set to His seal," or "bear witness to His Word," when I preached. And I knew I had the right to expect it for Jesus Himself had given the promise. "The works that I do," He declared, "shall ye do also and greater works than these shall ye do." (John 14:12.)

Then one day I read the Acts of the Apostles to find out if God's servants in the early Church got results wherever they went. And I found as I read that they aimed at, worked for, expected, and never failed to get Fruit. Peter preached on the day of Pentecost and 3,000 responded to that first appeal. There was a definite Outcome. With Paul it was the same. Follow him from place to place, and wherever he goes churches spring up. See how repeatedly the results are noted throughout the book. "There were added unto them about 3,000 souls." (2:41.) "Many of them which heard the Word believed, and turned unto the Lord." (11:21.) "Much people was added unto the Lord." (11:24.) "A great multitude believed." (14:1.) "Some believed, of the devout Greeks a great multitude, and of the chief women not a few" (17:4.) "Many believed." (17:34.) "Some believed." (27:24.) And Paul was able to declare "what things God had wrought by his Ministry." (21:19.)

Oh, how far short I fell! How fearfully I had failed! Failed in the very thing for which God had called me in to the Ministry. How seldom I could write after having preached that "a great number believed and turned unto the Lord," or even that "some believed." Nor was it possible for me to declare with Paul "what things God had wrought by my Ministry."

God clearly and emphatically states that it is His will that every servant of His should bear Fruit. "I have chosen you and ordained you," he affirms, "that ye should go and bring forth Fruit." (John 15:16.) Too long was I content to sow and evangelize, using the excuse that I left the results with God, thinking I had then done my duty. When people are saved and greatly blessed they will say so, and if they don't there is reason to doubt the reality of an Outcome. George Whitefield sometimes received hundreds of letters after he had preached telling of blessings and conversions.

"Go into the public assembly with a design to strike, and persuade some souls there, into repentance and salvation. Go to open blind eyes, to unstop deaf ears, to make the lame walk, to make the foolish wise, to raise those that are dead in trespasses and sins to a Heavenly and Divine life, and to bring guilty rebels to return to the love and obedience of their Maker, by Christ Jesus the great Reconciler, that they may be pardoned and saved. Go to diffuse the savour of Christ and His gospel through a whole assembly and to allure souls to partake of His grace and glory." -Dr. Watts.

There are men who feel they have special talents for the edification of believers, and so they give themselves entirely to building up Christians in the Faith. This was where I was side-tracked. I felt that I had special gifts for teaching and speaking to young Christians on the Deeper Life, and so I prepared a number of addresses with the idea of devoting my time to this work, until God mercifully opened my eyes and showed me how far I was astray. There is nothing that will deepen Christian experience, edify believers and build them up in the Faith so rapidly and thoroughly as seeing souls saved. Deep Holy Spirit meetings, where the power of God is working mightily in the conviction and Salvation of sinners, will do more for Christians than the teaching of years without it. Such was the experience of David Brainerd. In writing of the Indians among whom he laboured, he says, "Many of these people have gained more doctrinal knowledge of Divine truths since God first visited them in June last, than could have been instilled into their minds by the most diligent use of proper and instructive means for whole years together, without such a Divine influence."

An incident is related of Wm. Bramwell: "Several local preachers," it states, "had said that their talents were not to awaken and arouse careless and impenitent sinners, but to build up believers in the Faith. Mr. Bramwell endeavoured to prove that such reasoning was frequently used as an apology for the loss of the life and powers of God. That although some preachers might have a peculiar talent for comforting and edifying believers, yet that Christ's true servants, those whom He sent into His vineyard, could do all sorts of work. They could plough, dig, plant, sow, water, etc., and he earnestly entreated the preachers not to be satisfied without seeing the fruit of their labours, in the awakening and conversion of sinners."

"The building up of believers in their most Holy Faith was a principal object of Mr. Smith's ministry; but he never considered this species of labour successful, except as its results were indicated in the conversion of sinners." - Life of John Smith.

"He most certainly and perfectly edifies believers who are most ardently and scripturally laborious for the conversion of sinners." - Life of John Smith.

Work among believers of itself will not suffice. It matters not how spiritual a church may profess to be. If souls are not saved something is radically wrong, and the professed spirituality is simply a false experience, a delusion of the devil. People who are satisfied to meet together simply to have a good time among themselves, are far away from God. Real spirituality always has an Outcome. There will be a yearning and a love for souls. We have gone to places that have a name of being very deep and spiritual, and have often found that it was all in the head, the heart was unmoved; and there was, not infrequently, unconfessed sin somewhere. "Having a form of Godliness but denying the power thereof." Oh, the pathos of it all! Let us then challenge our spirituality and ask what it produces; for nothing less than a genuine Revival in the Body of Christ, resulting in a true Awakening among the unsaved, will ever satisfy the heart of God.

CHAPTER III

SOUL TRAVAIL

WE read in Isaiah 66:8, that "as soon as Zion travailed she brought forth her children"; and this is the most fundamental element in the work of God. Can children be born without pain? Can there be birth without travail? Yet how many expect in the spiritual realm that which is not possible in the natural! Oh, my brethren, nothing, absolutely nothing short of soul-travail will bring forth spiritual children! Finney tells us that he had no words to utter, he could only groan and weep when pleading with God for a lost soul. That was true travail.

Can we travail for a drowning child; but not for a perishing soul? It is not hard to weep when we realize that our little one is sinking below the surface for the last time. Anguish is spontaneous then. Not hard to agonize when we see the casket containing all that we love on earth borne out of the home. Ah, no; tears are natural at such a time! But oh, to realize and know that souls, precious, never dying souls are perishing all around us, going out into the blackness of darkness and despair, eternally lost, and yet to feel no anguish, shed no tears, know no travail! How cold our hearts are! How little we know of the compassion of Jesus! And yet God can give us this, and the fault is ours if we do not have it.

Jacob, you remember, travailed until he prevailed. But oh, who is doing it to-day? Who is really travailing in prayer? How many, even of our most spiritual Christian leaders are content to spend a few minutes a day on their knees, and then pride themselves on the time they have given to God! We expect extraordinary results, and extraordinary results are quite possible; signs and wonders will follow, but only through extraordinary efforts in the spiritual realm. Hence, nothing short of continuous, agonizing pleading for souls, hours upon hours, days and nights of prayer, will ever avail. Therefore, "gird yourselves, and lament ye priests; howl, ye ministers of the altar: come, lie all night in sackcloth, ye ministers of my God. Sanctify ye a fast, call a solemn assembly, gather the elders and all the inhabitants of the land unto the house of the Lord your God, and cry unto the Lord." (Joel 1:13-14.) Ah, yes, Joel knew the secret. Let us then lay aside everything else, and "cry unto the Lord."

"We read in the biographies of our forefathers, who were most successful in winning souls, that they prayed for hours in private. The question therefore arises, can we get the same results without following their example? If we can, then let us prove to the world that we have found a better way; but if not, then in God's name let us begin to follow those who through faith and patience obtained the promise. Our forefathers wept and prayed and agonized before the Lord for sinners to be saved, and would not rest until they were slain by the Sword of the Word of God. That was the secret of their mighty success; when things were slack and would not move they wrestled in prayer till God poured out His Spirit upon the people and sinners were converted." - Samuel Stevenson.

All men of God have become men mighty in prayer. The sun never rose on China, we are told, without finding Hudson Taylor on his knees. No wonder the China Inland Mission has been so wonderfully owned of God!

Conversion is the operation of the Holy Spirit, and prayer is the power that secures that operation. Souls are not saved by man but by God, and since He works in answer to prayer we have no choice but to follow the Divine plan. Prayer moves the Arm that moves the world.

Prevailing prayer is not easy. Only those who have wrestled with the powers of darkness know how hard it is. Paul says that "we wrestle not against flesh and blood, but against principalities, against powers, against the rulers of the darkness of this world, against spiritual wickedness in high places." (Eph. 6:12.) And when the Holy Spirit prays it is "with groanings which cannot be uttered." (Rom. 8:26.)

Oh, how few find time for prayer! There is time for everything else, time to sleep and time to eat, time to read the newspaper and the novel, time to visit friends, time for everything else under the sun, but – no time for prayer, the most important of all things, the one great essential.

Think of Susannah Wesley who, in spite of the fact that she had nineteen children, found time to shut herself in her room for a full hour each day, alone with God. My friends, it is not so much a case of *finding* time as it is of *making* time. And we can make time if we will.

So important did the Apostles consider it that they would not even wait on tables, but said: "We will give ourselves continually to *prayer* and to the ministry of the Word." (Acts. 6:4.) Yet how many ministers are burdened with the financial side of the work, and how many officials expect them to bear it! No wonder their spiritual work is of such little account!

"And it came to pass in those days, that He went out into a mountain to pray and continued *all night* in prayer to God." (Luke 6:12.) Such is the record concerning the Son of God; and if it was necessary for Him how much more so for us! Oh, think of it! – "all night in prayer." How many times could that be written of us? Hence, His strength! Hence, our weakness!

How fervently do the prophets of old urge a life of prayer! Hear Isaiah as he exclaims: "Ye that make mention of the Lord, keep not silence, and give Him no rest, till He establish, and till He make Jerusalem a praise in the earth." (Isa. 62:6-7.)

"Let the priests, the ministers of the Lord, weep between the porch and the altar, and let them say, spare Thy people, O Lord, and give not Thine heritage to reproach, that the heathen should rule over them; wherefore should they say among the people, 'Where is their God?' " (Joel 2:15.)

And not only did they urge prayer, but they themselves prayed. Daniel says, "I set my face unto the Lord God, to seek by prayer and supplication, with fasting, and sackcloth, and ashes; and I prayed unto the Lord my God, and made my confession." (Dan. 9:3-4.) And Ezra also wielded the same mighty weapon in every time of difficulty. "I fell upon my knees," he says, "and spread out my hands unto the Lord my God." (Ezra 9:5.) Then follows his most remarkable prayer. The same method was followed by Nehemiah. "And it came to pass when I heard their words," he relates, "that I sat down and wept, and mourned certain days and fasted, and prayed before the God of Heaven." (Neh.1:4.)

Such was also the practice of the Early Church. When Peter was in prison it is stated that "prayer was made without ceasing of the Church unto God for him," and "many were gathered together praying."

And now, in closing, may we turn to the record of God's dealings with His honoured servants, and hear what they have to say about the secret of results. And oh, may He put upon us the burden of prayer and supplication that rested upon these mighty spiritual giants and filled them with such travail!

"John Livingstone spent the whole night prior to June 21, 1630 in prayer and conference, being designated to preach the next day. After he had been speaking for an hour and a half a few drops of rain disconcerted the people, but Livingstone, asking them if they had any shelter from the storm of God's wrath, went on another hour. There were about 500 converted on the spot." – Livingstone of Shotts.

"I once knew a minister who had a Revival fourteen winters in succession. I did not know how to account for it, till I saw one of his members get up during a prayer meeting and make a confession. 'Brethren,' said he, 'I have been long in the habit of praying every Saturday night till after midnight, for the descent of the Holy Ghost upon us. And now, brethren,' and he began to weep, 'I confess that I have neglected it for two or three weeks.' The secret was out. That minister had a praying church." - Chas, G. Finney.

"Prevailing, or effectual prayer is that prayer which attains the blessing that it seeks. It is that prayer which effectually moves God. The very idea of effectual prayer is that it effects its objects." - Chas. G. Finney.

"In a certain town there had been no Revival for many years;

the Church was nearly extinct, the youth were all unconverted and desolation reigned unbroken. There lived in a retired part of the town an aged man, a blacksmith by trade, and of so stammering a tongue that it was painful to hear him speak. On one Friday, as he was at work in his shop alone, his mind became greatly exercised about the state of the Church and of the impenitent. His agony became so great that he was induced to lay by his work, lock the shop door, and spend the afternoon in prayer.

He prevailed, and on the Sabbath called on the minister and desired him to appoint a 'conference meeting.' After some hesitation, the minister consented, observing however, that he feared few would attend. He appointed it the same evening at a large private house. When evening came, more assembled than could be accommodated in the house. All were silent for a time, until one sinner broke out in tears, and said if anyone could pray, would they pray for him. Another followed, and another, and still another, until it was found that persons from every quarter of the town were under deep conviction. And what was remarkable was that they all dated their conviction at the hour the old man was praying in his shop. A powerful Revival followed. Thus this old stammering man prevailed, and as a prince had power with God."
- Chas. G. Finney.

" 'I have pleaded with God this day for hours, in the wood, for souls; He will give them. I know His sign. I shall have souls to-night. Yours, I trust will be one.' Night came, and with it such a power as I had never felt. Cries for mercy rang all over the chapel. Before the sermon was done, I, with many others, fell upon my knees to implore salvation." One of Thos. Collins' Converts.

"I went to my lonely retreat among the rocks. I wept much as I besought the Lord to give me souls." - Thos. Collins.

"I spent Friday in secret fasting, meditation, and prayer for help on the Lord's Day. About the middle of the sermon a man cried out; at the cry my soul ran over. I fell to prayer, nor could we preach any more for cries and tears all over the chapel. We continued in intercessions, and salvation came." - Thos. Collins.

"He gave himself unto prayer. Woods and lonely wayside places became closets. In such exercises time flew unheeded. He stopped amid the solitary crags to pray, and Heaven so met him there that hours elapsed unconsciously. Strong in the might of such baptisms, he became bold to declare the cross, and willing to bear it." - Life of Thos. Collins.

"It loaded me down with great agony. As I returned to my room I felt almost as if I should stagger under the burden that was on my mind; and I struggled, and groaned, and agonized, but could not frame to present the case before God in words, but only in groans and tears. The spirit struggled within me with groanings that could not be uttered." - Chas. G. Finney.

"I proposed that we should observe a closet concert of prayer for the revival of God's work; that we should pray at sunrise, at noon, and at sunset, in our closets, and continue this for one week, when we should come together again and see what further was to be done. No other means were used. But the spirit of prayer was immediately poured out wonderfully upon the young converts. Before the week was out I learned that some of them, when they would attempt to observe this season of prayer, would lose all their strength and be unable to rise to their feet, or even stand upon their knees in their closets; and that some would be prostrate on the floor, and pray with unutterable groanings for the Outpourings of the Spirit of God. The Spirit was poured out and before the week ended all the meetings were thronged; and there was as much interest in religion, I think, as there has been at any time during the Revival." - Chas. G. Finney.

"I have often seen him come downstairs in the morning after spending several hours in prayer, with his eyes swollen with weeping. He would soon introduce the subject of his anxiety by saying, 'I am a broken-hearted man; yes, indeed, I am an unhappy man; not for myself, but on account of others. God has given me such a sight of the value of precious souls that I cannot live if souls are not saved. Oh give me souls, or else I die!' " - Life of John Smith.

"God enabled me to so agonize in prayer that I was quite wet with perspiration, though in the shade and the cool wind. My soul was drawn out very much from the world, for multitudes of souls." -- David Brainerd.

"Near the middle of the afternoon God enabled me to wrestle ardently in intercession for my friends. But just at night the Lord visited me marvellously in prayer. I think my soul never was in such an agony before. I felt no restraint; for the treasures of Divine grace were opened to me. I wrestled for my friends, for the ingathering of souls, for multitudes of poor souls, and for many that I thought were the children of God. I was in such an agony from sun, half an hour high, till near dark, that I was all over wet with sweat." - David Brainerd.

"I withdrew for prayer hoping for strength from above. In prayer I was exceedingly enlarged and my soul was as much drawn out as I ever remember it to have been in my life. I was in such anguish, and pleaded with so much earnestness and importunity, that when I rose from my knees I felt extremely weak and overcome. I could scarcely walk straight; my joints were loosed; the sweat ran down my face and body; and nature seemed as if it would dissolve." - David Brainerd.

"Prayer must carry on our work, as well as preaching. He does not preach heartily to his people who does not pray for them. If we do not prevail with God to give them repentance and faith, we are not likely to prevail with them to repent and believe." - Richard Baxter.

"Several members of Jonathan Edwards' church had spent the whole night in prayer before he preached his memorable sermon, 'Sinners in the Hands of an Angry God.' The Holy Ghost was so mightily poured out, and God so manifest in holiness and majesty during the preaching of that sermon, that the elders threw their arms around the pillars of the church and cried, 'Lord, save us, we are slipping down to hell!' "

"Almost every night there has been a shaking among the people; and I have seen nearly twenty set at liberty. I believe I should have seen many more, but I cannot yet find one pleading man. There are many good people; but I have found no wrestlers with

God. At two or three small places, we had cries for mercy; and several were left in a state of deep distress." - Wm. Bramwell.

"Where the result which he desired did not attend his own ministry, he would spend days and nights almost constantly on his knees, weeping and pleading before God; and especially deploring his own inadequacy to the great work of saving souls. He was at times when he perceived no movement in the church, literally in agonies; travailing in birth for precious souls, till he saw Christ magnified in their salvation." – Life of John Smith.

"If you spend several hours in prayer daily, you will see great things." - John Nelson.

"He made it a rule to rise out of bed about twelve o'clock, and sit up till two, for prayer and converse with God; then he slept till four; at which time he always rose." - Life of John Nelson.

"Be instant and constant in prayer. Study, books, eloquence, fine sermons, are all nothing without prayer. Prayer brings the spirit, the life, the power." - Memoir of David Stoner.

"I find it necessary to begin at five in the morning and to pray at all opportunities till ten, or eleven, at night." – Wm. Bramwell.

But must we go back to these mighty men of old? Are there not some today who will ask God to burden them? May we not even in this generation have a Revival in answer to faithful, believing, travailing, prevailing prayer? Oh, then, "Lord, teach us not *how* to pray, but *to* pray."

God of Revival, meet us now,
As on Thy Name we call;
Forgive our sin and hear our pray'r,
Let show'rs of blessing fall.

God of Revival, search our hearts
And make us pure within;
Burn out the dross and purify.
Lord, cleanse us from all sin.

God of Revival, make us one,
That we may work with Thee;
Help us to pray until at last
Thy mighty pow'r we see.

SOUL TRAVAIL

God of Revival, Love Divine,
Thy joy to us restore;
Pour out Thy Spirit as of old
And stir our hearts once more.

God of Revival, save, we pray,
Let not the sinner die;
0 make us witnesses for Thee,
For this we humbly cry.

O.J.S.

THE PASSION FOR SOULS

CHAPTER IV

POWER FROM ON HIGH

THE Holy Spirit is able to make the Word as successful now as in the days of the apostles. He can bring in souls by hundreds and thousands as well as by ones and twos. The reason why we are no more prosperous is that we have not the Holy Spirit with us in might and power as in early times.

"If we had the Spirit sealing our ministry with power it would signify very little about talent. Men might be poor and uneducated, their words might be broken and ungrammatical; but if the might of the Spirit attended them, the humblest evangelist would be more successful than the most learned of divines, or the most eloquent of preachers.

It is extraordinary power from God, not talent, that wins the day. It is extraordinary spiritual unction, not extraordinary mental power, that we need. Mental power may fill a chapel but spiritual power fills the church with soul anguish. Mental power may gather a large congregation, but only spiritual power will save souls. What we need is spiritual power." - Chas. H. Spurgeon.

"Let the Spirit be lacking, and there may be wisdom of words, but not the wisdom of God; the powers of oratory, but not the power of God; the demonstration of argument and the logic of the schools, but not the demonstration of the Holy Spirit, the all-convincing logic of His lightning flash, such as convinced Saul before the Damascus gate. When the Spirit was outpoured the disciples were all filled with power from on high, the most unlettered tongue could silence gainsayers, and with its new fire burn its way through obstacles as flames fanned by mighty winds sweep through forests." - Arthur T. Pierson.

"The ministers of the Gospel must have this power of the Holy Spirit, because otherwise they are not sufficient for the ministry. For no man is sufficient for the work of the ministry by any natural parts and abilities of his own, nor yet by any acquired parts of human learning and knowledge, but only by this power of the

Holy Spirit; till he be endued with this, notwithstanding all his other accomplishments, he is altogether insufficient. And therefore the very apostles were to keep silent, till they were endued with this power; they were to wait at Jerusalem, till they had received the promise of the Spirit, and not to preach till then.

If they have not this power of the Holy Spirit they have not power at all. And therefore, seeing the ministers of the Gospel have not power from beneath, they must have power from on high; seeing they have no fleshly power, they must have spiritual power; seeing they have no power from earth and from men, they must have power from heaven and from God: that is, the power of the Holy Spirit coming on them; or else they have no power at all." - Wm. Dell.

But who is in the Anointing to-day? Who has the experience? It is promised; it is indispensable, and yet we labour on without it, working in the flesh like the disciples who toiled all night and caught nothing. And just so will it be with us. An hour's work in the Spirit will accomplish more than a year's work in the flesh. And the Fruit will remain. "It is the Spirit that quickeneth; the flesh profiteth nothing." (John 6:63.) "That which is born of the flesh is flesh, and that which is born of the Spirit is Spirit." (John 3:6.) It is Holy Spirit Fruit we want, pure gold without alloy, and nothing less. Not the kind that comes undone, but the genuine article that stands the test of time and Eternity; the kind we find at the prayer meeting as well as the Sunday services. Is this the kind of Fruit we are bearing? Is there conviction, and do souls come through into the glorious liberty of the children of God?

But have we the Enduement of Power? I don't mean, have we "claimed it" and gone forth reckoning it ours, but, have we the experience? If there is no Outcome, we certainly have not. If we are Spirit-filled there will be Holy Spirit Fruit. Men will break down in our meetings and sob out their sins to God. Let us see the Fruit if we are to believe in the Anointing. "Ye shall receive Power." And when Peter got it, three thousand were saved. And so with John Smith, Samuel Morris, Chas. G. Finney and others - there was Fruit. This is the evidence, this is the test, and only this.

If I am a man of God, endued with power from on High, souls will break down under my preaching; if I am not, nothing out of the ordinary will take place. Let this be the test for every preacher. By this we stand or fall.

"I was powerfully converted on the morning of the 10th of October, 1821", writes Chas G. Finney. "In the evening of the same day I received overwhelming baptisms of the Holy Ghost, that went through me, as it seemed to me, body and soul. I immediately found myself endued with such power from on high that a few words dropped here and there to individuals were the means of their immediate conversion. My words seemed to fasten like barbed arrows in the souls of men. They cut like a sword. They broke the heart like a hammer. Multitudes can attest to this. Oftentimes a word dropped without my remembering. It would fasten conviction, and often result in almost immediate conversion. Sometimes I would find myself, in a great measure, empty of this power. I would go and visit, and find that I made no saving impression. I would exhort and pray, with the same result. I would then set apart a day for private fasting and prayer, fearing that this power had departed from me, and would inquire anxiously after the reason of this apparent emptiness. After humbling myself, and crying out for help, the power would return upon me with all its freshness. This has been the experience of my life.

This power is a great marvel. I have many times seen people unable to endure the Word. The most simple and ordinary statements would cut men off their seats like a sword, would take away their strength, and render them almost helpless as dead men. Several times it has been true in my experience that I could not raise my voice, or say anything in prayer or exhortation, except in the mildest manner, without overcoming them. This power seems sometimes to pervade the atmosphere of the one who is highly charged with it. Many times great numbers of persons in a community will be clothed with this power when the very atmosphere of the whole place seems to be charged with the life of God. Strangers coming into it and passing through the place will be instantly smitten with conviction of sin and in many instances converted to Christ. When Christians humble themselves and consecrate their all afresh to Christ, and ask for this power, they will often receive such a baptism that they will be instrumental in converting more souls in one day than in all their lifetime before. While Christians remain humble enough to retain this power, the work of conversion will go on, till whole communities and regions of country are converted to Christ. The same is true of the ministry."

Where is the soul anguish of by-gone days, the wounded conscience, the sleepless nights, the groans and cries, the awful conviction of sin, the sobs and tears of the lost? Would to God we might hear and see it in this generation!

And who is to blame, the hearer? Do we attribute it to his hardness of heart? Does the fault lie there? Ah no, my brethren, the fault is ours; we are to blame. Were we what and where we ought to be, the signs would still follow as in the days of old. Then should not every failure, every sermon that fails to break the people down, drive us to our knees and result in deep heart searching, and humiliation. Let us never blame the people. If our churches are cold and unresponsive, it is because we are cold. Like pastor like people.

Oh how many there are who have been robbed of their testimony or who have never known the power of the Holy Spirit in their work! Their service is ineffective and their witness bearing null and void, while they accomplish little or nothing for God. Oh yes, they go through the motions, and sometimes they are very active, but it is all in the energy of the flesh, and no spiritual results follow. Souls are not saved nor are believers edified and built up in the Faith. Their preaching produces no Fruit and their Ministry is a ghastly failure. Oh, what a disappointing experience!

But, thank God, this need not be, for "Ye shall receive power," is His promise, and "Tarry ye until ye be endued with power from on High," His command.

The passage in Acts 1:8 literally reads: "Ye shall receive the power of the Holy Spirit coming upon you." So that the Anointing or Enduement of Power is that experience which is the result produced by the Holy Spirit coming upon the believer and equipping him for service.

Such Anointings are only received in the soul-agonies of deep travailing prayer. The nights and days of agonizing prayer for the souls of men, the countless hours of intercession that we find in the life of David Brainerd, the mighty wrestlings with the spiritual powers of darkness, until the body is wet with perspiration, that were so common to John Smith - this is something that goes much further than present-day teaching, but it is the only thing that will produce the Fruit, and do the work of which we are speaking.

It is from these hours of prevailing prayer that we go forth to our work in the Anointing to wield the Sword of the Spirit with deadly effect. Prayer is the secret. There can be no substitute. And for each special work there must be a special Anointing. It is not merely a matter of yielding and believing now. Ah no! The glorious supernatural results that I am talking of are not obtained so easily. It costs and costs tremendously.

" 'They continued with one accord in prayer and supplication' Prayer earnest, prayer united, and prayer persevering, these are the conditions; and these being fulfilled, we shall assuredly be 'endued with Power from on High.' We should never expect that the Power will fall upon us just because we happen once to awake and ask for it. Nor have any community of Christians a right to look for a great Manifestation of the Spirit, if they are not all ready to join in supplication, and 'with one accord,' to wait and pray as if it were the concern of each one.

It is only by waiting before that throne of grace that we become endued with the Holy Fire; but he who waits there long and believingly will imbibe that Fire, and come forth from his communion with God, bearing tokens of where he has been. For the individual believer, and, above all, for every labourer in the Lord's vineyard, the only way to gain spiritual Power is by secret waiting at the throne of God, for the Baptism.

If thou, then, wouldst have thy soul surcharged with the Fire of God, so that those who come nigh to thee shall feel some mysterious influence proceeding out from thee, thou must draw nigh to the source of that Fire, to the throne of God and of the Lamb, and shut thyself out from the world -that cold world, which so swiftly steals our Fire away. Enter into thy closet, and shut to thy door, and there, isolated, before the throne, await the Baptism; then the Fire shall fill thee, and when thou comest forth, holy Power will attend thee, and thou shalt labour not in thine own strength, but 'in demonstration of the Spirit, and of Power.' " - Wm. Arthur.

There are many in a false experience who think they are in the Anointing when they are not. All I can say is that the evidence; the proof is lacking. If they were, there would be the same things happening that those who were truly Anointed always witnessed. If all the professed Baptisms and Fillings of the Holy Spirit in modern conventions were real, the whole country would be set on fire. Nay, if just one man or one woman received the Anointing, the towns and villages for miles around might be swept by a mighty Revival, and thousands brought under deep conviction of sin and made to cry for mercy. The proof of the Anointing is the Outcome. The evidence that the spirit of Elijah had fallen on Elisha was the fact that he, too, smote the waters of Jordan and they divided.

Why is it so hard to get? you ask. Why? Because God will not pour His Spirit on the flesh. He must do His work in us first, and generally it takes a long time, for we will not let Him have His way with us. The savour of our own name, love of praise, or some such sinful obstacle blocks Him at every turn. He cannot humble us; He is unable to break our hearts because we will not yield.

Or else, because He cannot trust us with so great an honour. He knows we will only make shipwreck of it. Oh, the sad, heart-rending incidents of men and women who were once used in mighty Revivals, and, in the Anointing of the Spirit, brought hundreds of souls to God, who lost that cherished blessing and worked in the flesh ever after, accomplishing little or nothing!

They counted it too lightly; they became puffed up and proud; they allowed some little sin to come in; the Holy Spirit was grieved, and they found themselves, like Samson of old, shorn of their strength. At one time when they preached, souls cried aloud for mercy under awful conviction. Now they beg and coax; the meetings are dead and cold, while only a handful respond, and even these, are not Holy Spirit Fruit.

It remains only to insert the testimonies of some who have received the Enduement of Power to convince us of the reality of the experience. And if God could give it to one or a dozen He can give it to all.

"For thirteen years," writes Evan Roberts, "I had prayed for the Spirit; and this is the way I was led to pray. William Davies, the deacon, said one night in the society: 'Remember to be faithful. What if the Spirit descended and you were absent? Remember Thomas! What a loss he had!

I said to myself: 'I will have the Spirit'; and through every kind of weather and in spite of all difficulties, I went to the meetings. Many times, on seeing other boys with the boats on the tide, I was tempted to turn back and join them. But, no, I said to myself: 'Remember your resolve,' and on I went. I went faithfully to the meetings for prayer throughout the ten or eleven years I prayed for a Revival. It was the Spirit that moved me thus to think."

At a certain morning meeting which Evan Roberts attended, the evangelist in one of his petitions besought that the Lord would "bend us." The Spirit seemed to say to Roberts: "That's what you need, to be bent." And thus he describes his experience: "I felt a living force coming into my bosom. This grew and grew, and I was almost bursting. My bosom was boiling. What boiled in me was that verse: 'God commending His love.' I fell on my knees with my arms over the seat in front of me; the tears and perspiration flowed freely. I thought blood was gushing forth." Certain friends approached to wipe his face. Meanwhile he was crying out, "0 Lord, bend me! Bend me!" Then suddenly the glory broke.

Mr. Roberts adds: "After I was bent, a wave of peace came

43

over me, and the audience sang, 'I hear Thy welcome voice.' And as they sang I thought about the bending at the Judgment Day, and I was filled with compassion for those that would have to bend on that day, and I wept.

Henceforth, the salvation of souls became the burden of my heart. From that time I was on fire with a desire to go through all Wales, and if it were possible, I was willing to pay God for the privilege of going."

Such was the experience of Evan Roberts, God's honoured instrument in the great Welsh Revival. Now let us listen to the testimonies of John Wesley and Christmas Evans:

"About three in the morning as we were continuing instant in prayer, the power of God came mightily upon us, insomuch that many cried out for exceeding joy, and many fell to the ground. As soon as we recovered a little from the awe and amazement at the presence of His Majesty, we broke out with one voice, 'We praise Thee, 0 God, we acknowledge Thee to be the Lord.' " - John Wesley.

"I was weary of a cold heart towards Christ and His sacrifice, and the work of His Spirit - of a cold heart in the pulpit, in secret prayer, and in study. Fifteen years previously, I had felt my heart burning within, as if going to Emmaus with Jesus.

On a day ever to be remembered by me, as I was climbing up towards Cader Idris, I considered it to be incumbent upon me to pray, however hard I felt in my heart, and however worldly the frame of my spirit was. Having begun in the name of Jesus, I soon felt, as it were, the fetters loosening, and the old hardness of heart softening, and, as I thought, mountains of frosts and snow dissolving - and melting within me.

This engendered confidence in my soul in the promise of the Holy Ghost. I felt my whole mind relieved from some great bondage; tears flowed copiously, and I was constrained to cry out for the gracious visits of God, by restoring to my soul the joys of His salvation; and that He would visit the churches of the saints, and nearly all the ministers in the principality prayed for by their names.

This struggle lasted for three hours: it rose again and again, like one wave after another, or a high flowing tide, driven by a strong wind, until my nature became faint by weeping and crying. Thus I resigned myself to Christ, body and soul, gifts and labours – all my life - every day, and every hour that remained for me." - Christmas Evans.

Now, apparently strengthened as by a new spirit, with "might in the inner man," he laboured with renewed energy and zeal; and new and singular blessings descended upon his labours. In two years, his ten preaching places in Anglesea were increased to twenty, and *six hundred converts* were added to the church under his immediate care.

> Oh for the Spirit's mighty power,
> The Unction from above!
> Oh for a gracious heav'nly shower,
> The fulness of God's love!
>
> This only this, our one great need,
> Naught else can e'er prevail;
> Thus for the Unction how we plead,
> It only can avail.
>
> Our sins to God we now confess;
> To Him we yield our all,
> Believing He will surely bless
> As on His Name we call.
>
> And so we give ourselves to prayer
> That God may make us meet;
> For He must first our hearts prepare,
> His work in us complete.
>
> Then shall men turn to Calv'ry's stream
> With burdened hearts of woe;
> Salvation then shall be our theme,
> And earth be Heav'n below …
>
> O.J.S.

THE PASSION FOR SOULS

CHAPTER V

CONVICTION OF SIN

THERE is one thing that was always prominent in the great Revivals of past days, viz., a deep and a true conviction of sin. And it is one of the vital elements that is lacking to-day.

Where there is genuine conviction of sin it is not necessary to urge, coax or press in the energy of the flesh; sinners will come without being forced; they will come because they must. Those who go home from the meeting unable to eat or sleep because of deep conviction do not need to be coaxed and urged to seek relief.

In the modern campaign the evangelist calls upon people to accept Christ, and rightly so. But oh, that we could hear sinners calling upon Christ to accept them! People take salvation today in such a cold, formal, matter-of-fact, business-like sort of way, that it appears as though they are doing God an honour in condescending to receive His offer of Redemption. Their eyes are dry, their sense of sin absent; there is not any sign of penitence and contrition. They look upon it as a manly thing to do. But oh, if there were conviction! If they came with hearts bowed down, yea! Broken and contrite, came with the cry of the guilt-laden soul: "God be merciful to me a sinner!" Came trembling, with the burning life and death question of the Philippian jailor: "What must I do to be saved?" - What converts they would be!

If we are to get Holy Spirit Fruit, God must prepare the ground; the Holy Spirit must convict of sin before men can truly believe. It is right to tell people to believe when God has done His work in their hearts, but first they must feel their need. Let us wait until the Spirit of God has done His part before we say: "Believe on the Lord Jesus Christ and thou shalt be saved." Let us first see the signs of conviction as in the case of the Philippian jailor. And when their anguish is so deep that they are forced to cry aloud: "What must I do to be saved?", then we will know that they are ready to be exhorted to trust and exercise faith in Christ.

"There is another Gospel, too popular in the present day, which

47

seems to exclude conviction of sin and repentance from the scheme of Salvation; which demands from the sinner a mere intellectual assent to the fact of his guilt and sinfulness, and a like intellectual assent to the fact and sufficiency of Christ's atonement; and such assent yielded, tells him to go in peace, and to be happy in the assurance that the Lord Jesus has made it all right between his soul and God; thus crying peace, peace, when there is no peace.

Flimsy and false conversions of this sort may be one reason why so many who assume the Christian profession dishonour God and bring reproach on the Church by their inconsistent lives, and by their ultimate relapses into worldliness and sin. Sin must be felt before it can be mourned. Sinners must sorrow before they can be comforted. True conversions are the great want of the times. Conversions such as were common once, and shall be again, when the Church shakes off her lethargy, takes hold upon God's strength, and brings down the ancient power. Then, as of old, sinners will quail before the terror of the Lord." - J.H. Lord.

Would we think of calling a doctor before we were sick? Do we urge people who are well and strong to hasten to the physician? Does the man who is swimming well beseech those on the shore to come and save him? Certainly not! But let sickness come, and at once we feel our need and a doctor is called. We know that we require a remedy. When we feel ourselves sinking below the surface, and realize that we are drowning, we will, then, soon call for help. And oh, the agony through which we pass as we find ourselves going down and know that unless someone saves us, we are lost and must perish!

So it is with a perishing soul. When a man is convicted of his lost condition he will cry out in the bitter anguish of his heart: "What must I do to be saved?" He will need no urging, no coaxing; it is a matter of life or death to him, and he will do anything to be saved.

It is this lack of conviction that results in a spurious Revival, and causes the work to come undone. It is one thing to hold up the hand and sign a decision card, but it is quite another thing to get saved. Souls must be brought into clear and abiding liberty if the work is to last. It is one thing to have hundreds of professed converts during the excitement of the campaign, but it is another thing to come back five years after and find them still there.

John Bunyan understood it well when he pictured a Christian with his great load of sin on his back, and described his exercise of soul until he got rid of his burden at the foot of the Cross.

God has placed His own value on His Word. He calls it a "Fire," a "Hammer" and a "Sword." Now fire burns; a blow from a hammer hurts; while a cut from a sword causes real pain. And when His Word is proclaimed in the power of the Anointing it will have exactly the same results. It will burn like fire, break like a hammer and pierce like a sword, and the spiritual or mental pain will be just as severe and real as the physical. And if not, - then there is something wrong either with the messenger or the message.

"Were a person who had committed an awful crime to be suddenly arrested; were his guilt brought home to his conscience by some messenger of justice, in the pointed language of Holy Writ, 'Thou art the man'; it would be perfectly natural for the culprit to turn pale, to falter in his speech, to tremble, and to present every symptom of real agony and distress. When Belshazzar, the proud Assyrian monarch, saw the appearance of a man's hand writing upon the plaster of the wall of his palace, 'his countenance was changed, and his thoughts troubled him, so that the joints of his loins were loosed and his knees smote one against another.' And the effects have never yet been deemed unnatural. Why, then, should it be thought strange to behold sinners, who have been powerfully awakened by the Spirit of God, who are so deeply convinced of the enormity of their crimes as to apprehend they are every moment in danger of dropping into the burning lake, who imagine that hell is moved from beneath to meet them at their coming, why should it be thought unnatural for such persons to discover outward symptoms of the alarming distress and agitation felt within?" - Memoir of Wm. Bramwell.

"About the middle of the sermon a man cried out. I fell to

prayer, nor could we preach any more for cries and tears all over the chapel." - Thos. Collins.

"A Quaker who stood by was not a little displeased at the dissimulation of these creatures, and was biting his lips and knitting his brows, when he dropped down as thunder-struck. The agony he was in was even terrible to behold. We besought God not to lay folly to his charge, and he soon lifted up his head and cried aloud, 'Now I know thou art a prophet of the Lord.' " - John Wesley.

"J.H. was a man of regular life and conversation, one that constantly attended public prayers and sacrament, and was zealous for the church, and against dissenters of every denomination. Being informed that people fell into strange fits at the societies, he came to see and judge for himself.

We were going home when one met us in the street, and informed us that J .H. was fallen raving mad. It seems he sat down to dinner, but had in mind first to end the sermon he had borrowed on Salvation by Faith. In reading the last page, he changed colour, fell off his chair, and began screaming terribly, and beating himself against the ground.

The neighbours were alarmed and flocked together to the house. Between one and two I came in and found him on the floor, the room being full of people whom his wife would have kept without, but he cried out aloud, 'No, let them all come, let all the world see the just judgment of God.' Two or three men were holding him as best they could. He immediately fixed his eyes upon me, and stretching out his hand cried, 'Aye, this is he whom I said was a deceiver of the people. But God has overtaken me. I said it was all a delusion. But this is no delusion.'

We all betook ourselves to prayer; his pangs ceased and both his body and soul were set at liberty." - John Wesley.

"The power of God seemed to descend upon the assembly like a mighty, rushing wind, and with an astonishing energy bore down all before it. I stood amazed at the influence, which seized the audience almost universally; and could compare it to nothing more apt than the irresistible force of a mighty torrent or a swelling deluge that with its insupportable weight and pressure bears down and sweeps before it whatever comes in its way. Almost all persons of all ages were bowed down with concern together, and scarcely one was able to withstand the shock of this surprising operation: Old men and women, who had been drunken wretches for many years and some little children, not more than six or seven years of age, appeared in distress for their souls, as well as persons of middle age.

The most stubborn hearts were now obliged to bow. A principal man among the Indians, who, before, was most secure and self-righteous, and thought his state good, because he knew more than the generality of the Indians had formerly done, and who with a great degree of confidence the day before told me he had been a Christian more than ten years, was now brought under solemn concern for his soul and wept bitterly. Another man, advanced in years, who had been a murderer, a conjurer, and a notorious drunkard, was likewise brought now to cry for mercy with many tears, and to complain much that he could be no more concerned when he saw his dangers so very great.

They were almost universally praying and crying for mercy in every part of the house, and many out of doors, and numbers could neither go nor stand. Their concern was so great, each one for himself, that none seemed to take any notice of those about them, but each prayed freely for himself." - David Brainerd. .

"The chapel was crowded to excess. The Word was 'quick and powerful,' numbers 'were pricked in their hearts,' and in the agony of conviction cried mightily for mercy. The sermon was followed by a prayer meeting. Midnight arrived and the penitents were still upon their knees, resolved to plead till they prevailed. As one and another found peace through believing and withdrew, others whose hearts were stricken filled their places. So intense was the Awakening, that though the Squire had retired, the alarmed and sorrowing people could not be induced to leave the chapel, but all night through, and all through the following day and night, the prayer meeting continued without intermission. It was supposed that over one hundred persons were converted, whilst many an old professor received quickening and gave himself to God by a fuller consecration." - Memoir of Squire Brooke.

"While engaged in prayer, two of those who came in were awakened and began to cry for mercy." - Wm. Carvosso.

"While I was praying, the power of God descended and he and his penitent companion were cut to the heart and wept aloud for their sins." - Wm. Carvosso.

"When the conviction as to its mental process reaches its crisis, the person, through weakness, is unable to sit or stand, and either kneels or lies down. A great number of convicted persons in this town and neighbourhood, and now I believe in all directions in the north where the Revival prevails, are 'smitten down' as suddenly and they fall as nerveless and paralysed and powerless, as if killed instantly by a shotgun. They fall with a deep groan, some with a wild cry of horror - the greater number with the intensely earnest plea, 'Lord Jesus, have mercy on my soul!' The whole frame trembles like an aspen leaf, an intolerable weight is felt upon the chest, a choking sensation is experienced and relief from this found only in the loud, urgent prayer for deliverance. Usually the bodily distress and mental anguish continue till some degree of confidence in Christ is found. Then the look, the tone, the gestures, instantly change. The aspect of anguish and despair is changed for that of gratitude, and triumph, and adoration. The language and the looks, and terrible struggles, and loud desperate depreciation, tell convincingly, as the parties themselves declare, that they are in deadly conflict with the old serpent. The perspiration rolls off the anguished victims; their very hair is moistened. Some pass through this exhausting conflict several times; others but once. There is no appetite for food; many will eat nothing for a number of days. They do not sleep, though they may lie down with their eyes shut." - The Irish Revival, 1859.

"The power of the Lord's Spirit became so mighty upon their souls as to carry all before it, like the rushing mighty wind of Pentecost. Some were screaming out in agony; others - and among these strong men - fell to the ground as if they had been dead. I was obliged to give out a psalm, our voices mingled with the mourning and groans of many prisoners sighing for deliverance." - Wm. Burns.

"A Revival always includes conviction of sin on the part of the church. Back-slidden professors cannot wake up and begin right away in the service of God without deep searchings of heart. The fountains of sin need to be broken up. In a true Revival, Christians are always brought under such conviction; they see their sins in such a light that often they find it impossible to maintain a hope of their acceptance with God.

It does not always go to that extent, but there are always, in a genuine Revival, deep convictions of sin, and often cases of abandoning all hope." - Chas. G. Finney.

Save, Lord, I pray, oh save to-day.
Convict and save from sin;
Break hardened hearts, give penitence,
Go Spirit, bring them in.

Pour out Thy Spirit, Lord, I pray;
Now let Him fall and save
The high and low. the rich and poor
Their precious souls I crave.

May deep distress and agony
Fall now on one and all,
Till, born again thro' Jesus' blood,
Souls at Thy altar call.

Save Lord, I pray, oh save the lost
Ere Jesus comes again;
Spirit of God, still strive and plead,
Or some will weep in vain.

Spirit Divine, take not Thy flight.
Nor let the sinner die;
Death hovers near, night cometh fast
Hear Thou Thy servant's cry

O.J.S.

CHAPTER VI

OBSTACLES TO REVIVAL

THERE is only one obstacle that can block up the channel and choke God's power, and that is SIN. Sin is the great barrier. It alone can hinder the work of the Spirit and prevent a Revival. "If I regard iniquity in my heart," declared David, "the Lord will not hear me" (Psalm 66:18). And in Isaiah 59:1-2, we have these significant words: "Behold, the Lord's hand is not shortened, that it cannot save; neither His ear heavy, that it cannot hear: but your iniquities have separated between you and your God, and your sins have hid His face from you, that He will not hear." Sin, then, is the great barrier, and it must be put away. Nor is there any alternative. There can be no compromise. God will not work as long as there is iniquity covered up.

In Hosea 10:12 we read, "Sow to yourselves in righteousness, reap in mercy; break up your fallow ground: for it is time to seek the Lord, till He come and rain righteousness upon you." And in 2 Chronicles 7:14 the promise of blessing is vouchsafed, based, however, upon unalterable conditions: "If my people, which are called by my name," declares the Lord, "shall humble themselves, and pray, and seek my face, and turn from their wicked ways; *then* will I hear from heaven, and will forgive their sin, and will heal their land." Hence, nothing short of a broken heart over sin, full confession and restitution, will satisfy God. Sin must be forsaken utterly.

And not only sorrow for the consequences and punishment of sin, but for sin itself as committed against God. Hell is full of remorse, but only for the punishment incurred. There is no real contrition. The rich man uttered not a word of sorrow for his sin against God (Luke 16:29-30). But David, though guilty of both murder and adultery, saw his sin as against God alone (Psalm 5I:4). Mere remorse is not true Godly sorrow unto repentance. Judas, though filled with remorse, never repented.

Now God alone is able to bestow a contrite and broken heart, a sorrow that will result in the confession and forsaking of sin. And nothing short of that will suffice. "The sacrifices of God are a broken spirit; a broken and a contrite heart, O God, Thou wilt not despise." (Psalms 51:17) "He that covereth his sins shall not prosper: but whoso confesseth and forsaketh them shall find mercy." (Prov. 28:13) "Only acknowledge thine iniquity that thou hast transgressed against the Lord Thy God." (Jer. 3:13)

It is a common experience to find souls kneeling at the altar and calling upon God with apparent great anguish of heart, who fail to receive anything. And it is just as common for groups of people to gather together for nights of prayer for a Revival and yet never have their prayers answered. What is the trouble? Let the Word of God answer: "Your iniquities have separated between you and your God and your sins have hid His face from you, that He will not hear." Hence, let us uncover our sin first of all; let us make straight the crooked ways, let us gather out the stones, and then we may ask in faith and expectancy for showers of blessing.

Now let us take our sins one by one and deal with each transgression separately. And let us ask ourselves the following questions. It may be we are guilty and God will speak to us.

(1) Have we *forgiven* everyone? Is there any malice, spite, hatred or enmity in our hearts? Do we cherish grudges; and have we refused to be reconciled?

(2) Do we get *angry?* Are there any uprisings within? Is it true that we still lose our temper? Does wrath hold us at times in its grip?

(3) Is there any feeling of *jealousy?* When another is preferred before us, does it make us envious? Do we get jealous of those who can pray, speak and do things better than we can?

(4) Do we get *impatient* and *irritated?* Do little things vex and annoy? Or are we sweet, calm and unruffled under all circumstances?

(5) Are we *offended* easily? When people fail to notice us and pass by without speaking, does it hurt? If others are made much of and we are neglected, how do we feel about it?

(6) Is there any *pride* in our hearts? Are we puffed up? Do we

think a great deal of our own position and attainments?

(7) Have we been *dishonest?* Is our business open and above reproach? Do we give a yard for a yard and a pound for a pound?

(8) Have we been *gossiping* about people? Do we slander the characters of others? Are we talebearers and busybodies?

(9) Do we *criticize* unlovingly, harshly, severely? Are we always finding fault and looking for the flaws in others?

(10) Do we *rob* God? Have we stolen time that belongs to Him? Has our money been withheld?

(11) Are we *worldly?* Do we love the glitter, the pomp, and the show of this life?

(12) Have we *stolen?* Do we take little things that do not belong to us?

(13) Do we harbour a spirit of *bitterness* towards others? Is there hatred in our hearts?

(14) Are our lives filled with *lightness* and *frivolity?* Is our conduct unseemly? Would the world by our actions consider us on its side?

(I5) Have we wronged anyone and failed to make *restitution?* Or, has the spirit of Zacchaeus possessed us? Have we restored the many little things that God has shown us?

(16) Are we *worried* or *anxious?* Do we fail to trust God for our temporal and spiritual needs? Are we continually crossing bridges before we come to them?

(17) Are we guilty of *immorality?* Do we allow our minds to harbour impure and unholy imaginations?

(I8) Are we *true* in our statements, or do we exaggerate and thus convey false impressions? Have we lied?

(I9) Are we guilty of the sin of *unbelief?* In spite of all He has done for us, do we still refuse to believe His Word? Do we murmur and complain?

(20) Have we committed the sin of *prayerlessness?* Are we intercessors? Do we pray? How much time are we spending in prayer? Have we crowded prayer out of our lives?

(2I) Are we neglecting *God's Word?* How many chapters do we read each day? Are we Bible students? Do we draw our source of supply from the Scriptures?

(22) Have we failed to *confess* Christ openly? Are we ashamed of Jesus? Do we keep our mouths closed when we are surrounded by worldly people? Are we witnessing daily?

(23) Are we *burdened* for the salvation of souls? Have we a love for the lost? Is there any compassion in our hearts for those who are perishing?

(24) Have we lost our first love and are we no longer on fire for God?

These are the things, both negative and positive, that prevent the work of God in the midst of His people. Let us be honest and call them by their right name. "SIN" is the word that God uses. And the sooner we admit that we have sinned and are ready to confess and forsake it, the sooner may we expect God to hear us and work in mighty power. Why deceive ourselves? We cannot deceive God. Then let us remove the obstacle, the hindering thing before we take another step. "If we would judge ourselves we should not be judged." "Judgment must begin at the house of God."

This has been the history of revival work all down the centuries. Night after night sermons have been preached and no results obtained, until some elder or deacon bursts out in an agony of confession, and, going to the one whom he has wronged, craves forgiveness. Or some woman who is a prominent worker breaks down and in tears confesses publicly that she has been gossiping about some other sister or is not on speaking terms with the person across the aisle. Then when confession and restitution have been made, the fallow ground broken up, and sin uncovered and acknowledged, then and not until then, the Spirit of God comes upon the audience and a Revival sweeps over the community.

Generally there is but one sin, one hindering thing. It was an Achan in the camp of Israel. And God will put His finger directly on the spot. Nor will He take it off until that one obstacle has been dealt with.

Oh then, let us plead first of all the prayer of David when he cried, "Search me, O God, and see if there be any wicked way in me." And no sooner will the obstacle of sin be taken out of the way than God will come in mighty revival power.

OBSTACLES TO REVIVAL

A city full of churches,
Great preachers, lettered men,
Grand music, choirs and organs;
If these all fail, what then?
Good workers, eager, earnest,
Who labour hour by hour;
But where, oh where, my brother,
Is God's Almighty power?

Refinement: education!
They want the very best.
Their plans and schemes are perfect.
They give themselves no rest;
They get the best of talent,
They try their uttermost,
But what they need, my brother,
Is God the Holy Ghost!

We may spend time and money
And preach from wisdom's lore
But education only
Will keep God's people poor.
God wants not worldly wisdom,
He seeks no smiles to win;
But what is needed, brother,
Is that we deal with sin!

It is the Holy Spirit
That quickeneth the soul.
God will not take man-worship,
Nor bow to man's control.
No human innovation,
No skill. or worldly art,
Can give a true repentance.
Or break the sinner's heart.

We may have human wisdom,
Grand singing, great success:
There may be fine equipment,
But these things do not bless.
God wants a pure, clean vessel,
Anointed lips and true.
A man filled with the Spirit,
To speak His message through.

59

THE PASSION FOR SOULS

Great God, revive us truly!
And keep us every day;
That men may all acknowledge,
We live just as we pray.
The Lord's hand is not shortened.
He still delights to bless,
If we depart from evil
And all our sins confess.

Note: The above poem was written by Samuel Stevenson who first introduced me to some of the revivalists and prayer-warriors I have mentioned, and taught me many of these great truths.

CHAPTER VII

FAITH FOR REVIVAL

FAITH is the key that unlocks the door of God's power. "By faith the walls of Jericho fell down." And in revival work one of the indispensable prerequisites is a living, vital Faith. "All things are possible to him that believeth."

The man who is to be used of the Lord will hear from Heaven. God will give him a promise. Not the general promises of the Word that apply to so many of His children, but a definite, unmistakable message direct to his own heart. Some familiar promise, it may be, will suddenly grip him in such a way that he will know God has spoken. Hence, if I would attempt a new work for God, let me ask myself first of all the questions: "Have I a promise? Has God spoken?"

It was this divine assurance that enabled the prophets of old to go to the people and declare, "Thus saith the Lord." And until God has so commissioned us, we had better remain on our faces in prayer, lest He say: "Woe to the prophets that run, and I have not sent them!" But when a man has heard from God, then, "though it tarry, wait for it; because it will surely come." And even should years intervene, yet will God fulfill His Word.

And oh, the joy of hearing and recognizing that voice! What encouragement! What faith! How the heart leaps within! No questioning then. No guessing and wondering after that. For days, for weeks it may be, there has been the earnest pleading in prayer as to God's will. Then from His Word, or by the Holy Spirit, there comes His message, and all is perfect rest. Not that the thing is done or the expectation realized; but God has spoken, and there can no longer be any doubt. "He will bring it to pass."

I saw, in days gone by, a vision of a great work in the city of Toronto, and I prayed about it that I might know the mind of the Lord. At last, one day, He spoke. Yea, a second time came His assuring Word. Forthwith I waited, waited in prayer and faith, knowing that He would surely bring it to pass. Three years went by, years of fearful testing. Without His promise I would have gone down, my high hopes scattered to the winds, but God had spoken, and I had only to pray: "Do as Thou hast said." Finally, when three full years had passed, He established the work of which He had spoken.

An incident is told of a place called Filey, in the early days of Methodism, to which preacher after preacher had been sent, but all to no purpose. The village was a stronghold of satanic power, and each one in turn had been driven out, until at last it was decided to give it up as a hopeless task.

Just before the matter was finally settled, however, the now famous John Oxtoby, or "Praying Johnny" as he was called, begged the Conference to send him, and so let the people have one more chance. They agreed, and a few days afterwards John set out on his journey. On the way a person who knew him inquired where he was going. "To Filey," was the reply, "where the Lord is going to revive His work."

As he drew near the place, on ascending the hill between Muston and Filey, suddenly a view of the town burst upon his sight. So intense were his feelings that he fell upon his knees under a hedge and wrestled and wept and prayed for the success of his mission. We have been told that a miller, who was on the other side of the hedge, heard a voice and stopped in astonishment to listen, when he heard Johnny say, "Thou munna mak a feal o' me! Thou munna mak a feal o' me! I told them at Bridlington that Thou was going to revive Thy work, and Thou must do so, or I shall never be able to show my face among them again, and then what will the people say about praying and believing?"

He continued to plead for several hours. The struggle was long and heavy, but he would not cease. He made his very weakness and inefficiency a plea. At length, the clouds dispersed, the glory filled his soul, and he rose exclaiming, "It is done, Lord. It is done. Filey is taken! Filey is taken!"

And taken it was, and all in it, and no mistake. Fresh from the Mercy-seat he entered the place, and commenced singing up the streets, "Turn to the Lord and seek salvation," etc. A crowd of stalwart fishermen flocked to listen. Unusual power attended his address, hardened sinners wept, strong men trembled, and while he prayed, over a dozen of them fell on their knees, and cried aloud for mercy and found it.

Well now, do we know what it is to offer the prayer of Faith? Have we ever prayed thus? "I knew a father," writes Chas. G. Finney, "who was a good man, but had erroneous views respecting the prayer of faith; and his whole family of children were grown up, without one of them being converted. At length his son sickened, and seemed about to die. The father prayed, but the son grew worse, and seemed sinking into the grave without hope. The father prayed, until his anguish was unutterable. He went at last and prayed (there seemed no prospect of his son surviving) so that he poured out his soul as if he would not be denied, till at length he got an assurance that his son would not only live but be converted; and that not only this one, but his whole family would be converted to God. He came into the house, and told his family his son would not die. They were astonished at him. 'I tell you,' said he, 'he will not die. And no child of mine will ever die in his sins.' That man's children were all converted years ago."

"A clergyman once told me of a revival among his people, which commenced with a zealous and devoted woman in the Church. She became anxious about sinners, and gave herself to praying for them; she prayed, and her distress increased; and she finally came to the minister, and talked with him, asking him to appoint an anxious inquirers' meeting, for she felt that one was needed. The minister put her off, for he felt nothing of any such need. The next week she came again, and besought him again to appoint such a meeting. She knew there would be somebody to come, for she felt as if God was going to pour out His Spirit. The minister once more put her off. And finally she said to him: 'If you do not appoint the meeting I shall die, for there is certainly going to be a revival.' The next Sabbath he appointed a meeting, and said that if there were any who wished to converse with him about the salvation of their souls, he would meet them on such an evening. He did not know of one, but when he went to the place, to his astonishment he found a large number of anxious inquirers."

- Chas. G. Finney.

"The first ray of light that broke in upon the midnight which rested on the Churches in Oneida County, in the fall of 1825, was from a woman in feeble health, who, I believe, had never been in a powerful revival. Her soul was exercised about sinners. She was in an agony for the land. She did not know what ailed her, but she kept praying more and more, till it seemed as if her agony would destroy her body. At length she became full of joy, and exclaimed: 'God has come! God has come! There is no mistake about it, the work is begun, and is going all over the region.' And sure enough the work began, and her family were all converted, and the work spread all over that part of the country." - Chas. G. Finney.

This, then, is the secret - Faith, the Faith of Hebrews eleven, the Faith of God, His gift, based on His Word, direct to the heart of His servant. Such Faith will remove mountains, and accomplish the impossible. Not the presumptuous faith that believes without the evidence of the Spirit, and costs nothing, and then when time elapses and things do not come to pass, rapidly fades away; but the Faith of God, born in the agony of prevailing prayer and soul travail. This Faith will rise above the storms of discouragement and adversity, will triumph over time, and continue to burn brightly while waiting for the accomplishment of its object. Oh for such a Faith to-day!

"Faith. mighty faith. the promise sees,
And looks to God alone;
Laughs at impossibilities
And cries, 'It shall be done!'

The thing surpasses all my thought;
But faithful is my Lord;
Through unbelief I stagger not,
For God hath spoke the word.

That mighty faith on me bestow
Which cannot ask in vane;
Which holds and will not let Thee go,
Till I my suit obtain."

O.J.S

CHAPTER VIII

HUNGER FOR REVIVAL

WHEN I visited the Russian Mission Fields of Europe, in 1924, 1929 and 1936, I saw God working in revival power. People would walk thirty miles, or drive with horses and wagons two hundred miles, to attend meetings. Services lasted three hours or longer, and in some cases, three services were held each day, and then the people complained that they were not getting enough. In one place they met in a meeting of their own in the early morning hours, before even the workers appeared on the scene, making four services in all each day.

No need to spend money on advertising. One told another, and everybody came, until they were standing in the aisles, sitting in every available space on the platform and crowding the largest auditoriums so that scarcely another person could squeeze in. Well do I remember preaching to three thousand in a Lutheran Church. Oh, how they listened! Yes, and in the open air it was the same. For three hours I have seen them stand in the rain - men, women and children - so hungry were they.

And oh, how God worked! From the very commencement the spirit of Revival was in the air. They prayed, sang and testified, the tears streaming down their cheeks. With stricken hearts they listened to the messages. When the invitation was given, they flocked to the front, and falling on their knees, their eyes overflowing with tears, cried to God for mercy. Pastor Wm. Fetler was my interpreter, and what an inspiration he was! But let me quote from my diary - it will better illustrate what I mean:

"To describe the scenes that have been enacted by the Holy Ghost would be simply impossible; for what God has wrought is nothing less than miraculous. Each night the great auditorium was literally thronged, and, during the closing days, crowded beyond capacity, gallery, platform and all, with people standing everywhere. Night after night souls came forward for salvation, and the altar was filled over and over again. Great numbers accepted Christ for the first time. How many I do not know.

But the ten o'clock morning meeting was the great time of the feast. The first morning, the main auditorium below was full, with a few in the choir seats. The second day there were more, and the third still more, and a glorious break began. But on the fourth morning there was no room. The choir seats were filled. Extra chairs were then placed on the platform and wherever there was space. Still the people came, until, at last, many were compelled to stand in the aisles. Then the power of God fell on the audience. Men and women knelt everywhere, and oh, such prayers! Such tears! Such penitence and confession! Such joy and peace! Such testimonies! And how they sang! Truly, it was Heaven on earth.

At the close of the meeting, there came a call for another, an extra, in the afternoon at four. Would I preach again? I consented, and at four they were back. Once more, the power of God was present. Tears flowed freely. Joy unspeakable and glory was depicted on many a countenance. In silence we knelt before God, and into numbers of lives the Spirit came. At six-thirty I preached again, and also at eight - four times in one day.

Soon after I retired to my room there was a knock on the door. One of the students entered. He told me how God had spoken to him. He described his great hunger of heart. 'I have determined to pray all night,' he said, 'for I will not cease until I know the power of the Holy Ghost in my life.' We prayed together, and he sobbed aloud. Thus the break started.

A few minutes later there came another knock. Would I meet with some in an adjoining room? I went. When I entered I found a group from the office on their faces. To them also God had spoken. Prayer again, agonizing, definite prayer, ascended to God. Sin was dealt with and put away, and a full surrender made, for once more the Holy Spirit had His way.

Presently in troops all the students in a body, and kneeling down, in Russian, German, Lettish and English, they poured our their hearts to God. Oh, what a melting time! How they wept before the Lord! What a joy it was to be in such an atmosphere of Revival and to see the Holy Spirit Himself at work. Finally, they left, left to continue in prayer in their own rooms; how late I do not know. And at twelve o'clock I returned to my office, and with joy and gratitude in my soul, went to bed. What a blessed day it had been!

Next morning we were compelled to move to the main auditorium, for more than twelve hundred were present, and again the altar was packed. Praise God! At four o'clock I preached again, this time to an audience of over fifteen hundred, many being compelled to stand. Once more the altar was lined with souls. Then, at seven o'clock, I faced my third congregation, and the power of the Spirit was most real. There was a holy hush on the large audience, so that at the close, so many came forward that the After-Meeting lasted an hour. This was in the lower hall.

At eight I went upstairs and found an audience of thirteen hundred waiting for me. I again proclaimed the Message and gave the invitation, and immediately a long row of men and women, young and old, stood at the altar and, with contrition and joy, accepted Christ. That was my fourth service for the day, and I thought my last; but when I returned to the Mission House I found a room full of Russians, all on their faces before God, praying quietly, earnestly, as only Russians can. For a while I joined them, then left, and at twelve o'clock went to bed. What a day it had been! What meetings! What marvellous conversions! What joy! What power! Never in my life have I preached to such congregations neither in Canada nor in the United States.

Easter Sunday was a never-to-be-forgotten day. The first service was at six in the morning. The night before I had attended the Greek Orthodox Service at midnight, had seen the people with their candles, had watched the priests in their gorgeous robes as they marched three times around the church outside, had listened to the wonderful singing of the choir, and had heard the sermon of the Archbishop on the Resurrection. It was two o'clock when I got to bed. Hence, to preach at six in the morning was not easy. There were twelve hundred present. Many responded to the invitation and accepted Christ.

At ten o'clock I preached again to a congregation of sixteen hundred. Even the aisles in the gallery were full, and people were standing everywhere. It was a marvellous scene. The meeting lasted for four hours.

After dinner I threw myself on my bed and fell asleep, waking just in time for the next service, at four. There were fourteen hundred present. A great number came forward for salvation as the Spirit of God moved in awe-inspiring power on the audience. Tears flowed down many cheeks. Men stood wiping their swollen eyes. Salvation had come to many a heart, and, with joy beaming on their faces, they warmly pressed my hand as I walked down the long line of converts. There were young men and women there. Older ones too. Many with grey hair. A few little children. All had sought and many found the Saviour. Oh what boundless joy!

On Monday I was in a Russian church, where, nearly five years before, I had preached the Gospel. Here at ten o'clock I found a crowded audience, men and women bending down from the gallery at the side and away at the back, people standing here and there, a great massed choir and band behind me. I spoke with conviction on victory over sin, and at the close scores knelt as the blessed Holy Spirit entered their lives and made the transaction real. God mightily worked. Many of their faces seemed literally glorified, so great was their joy.

In another Russian city our first service was held in the local church, which was but half full, yet there was the beginning of a break at once. Many prayed with tears. At the next service the church was packed, with people standing. Our third was held in an auditorium seating three thousand, so it was stated, but it proved to be too small. So great was the crowd, and so deep the interest, that numbers were compelled to stand throughout. In spite of the huge throng, many came forward and knelt at the altar to accept Christ, and deep conviction settled on the congregation.

Then came Monday night. Would the great crowd still come? Or would Monday over here be what it is in America? The question was soon answered, for, upon reaching the church, we found it packed to the roof, with numbers standing in the aisles. Oh what a sight! Two galleries, one far back, above the first.

Tense faces gazing down upon us. How my soul was stirred as I watched them! And oh, how they listened! At the close I called for an After Meeting. About five hundred left; the rest would not. And so, with some twenty-five hundred present, I had to proceed. Quickly the front seats were filled with seekers. Carefully I explained the Gospel. As I spoke tears flowed down their cheeks. Soon they were on their knees. Sins were confessed and forgiven, Christ received, and notes of praise offered to God. Oh how changed their countenances when they arose! How their eyes glistened with joy!

Thus ended one of the most wonderful series of revival meetings I have ever held. Never in America have I had just such an experience. Nor will I ever forget the glorious scenes in which I participated. What spiritual hunger and thirst after God! Where, in Canada, can it be duplicated? My whole soul goes out to these great multitudes. How marvellously God visited them! Oh how I praise Him! Glory be to His matchless Name forever! He is still the same. The God of Wesley and Finney, the God of Moody and Evan Roberts -- this God is our God even forever and ever. He is still the God of Revival. His hand has never been shortened nor His ear become heavy. He hears, He answers prayer. Hallelujah!

As for myself, I feel deeply humbled. God has richly blessed my own soul. It has meant a new crucifixion, a deeper experience, and a closer walk. My heart has been melted again and again. Henceforth, as never before, it must be 'God first.' My own plans and ambitions I joyfully set aside; His I accept. What the future holds I know not, but my times are in His hands. If only He will condescend to use me in deep, spiritual revival work, I will be more than satisfied; it matters not where, here or at home. 'Where He leads me, I will follow.' I desire to be utterly abandoned to God, and to live every moment in a realm so far above the world and the flesh that I will dwell in unbroken communion and uninterrupted fellowship with my blessed Lord."

My friends, I have travelled through Europe, the Near and the Far East, Canada and the United States. I have gone from the Atlantic to the Pacific, and from the Gulf of Mexico to the Great

Lakes, again and again. I have attended the best evangelistic meetings, and listened to the greatest Evangelists and Bible Teachers on the continent. But I have never, anywhere, seen duplicated what I have just described, except under the ministry of those who are working in Russian lands.

And why? What is the explanation? Has God forsaken America? Is He through with Canada? Has England had her chance? Why are there no Revivals anywhere in these countries today? Simply because the supreme prerequisite for Revival is lacking. That which I saw in continental Europe, I have yet to see here, namely, *hunger*. My friends, there is no real, true, deep, spiritual hunger in this country; no heart-searching after God. *Things* fill our vision. We have so many comforts and even luxuries that we do not feel our need of God. If we were to be stripped of almost everything we possess it might prove to be our salvation.

People here do not want to attend meetings. Oftentimes it takes hundreds of dollars' worth of advertising to even interest them. The theatres and moving picture shows are thronged; the dance halls, beaches and parks crowded, but our churches, for the most part, are empty. People would never dream of walking even two miles to attend a service; nor would they stand for three hours in the open air to hear the Gospel. Hence my diagnosis that there is no *hunger*. The nicer the day, the greater the temptation for an auto ride. God must take second or third place. The Russian people have but little of this world's goods: hence their spiritual hunger for the riches of God.

Let us, those of us who have a hunger - and, thank God, there are a few here and there - let us take up a lamentation for the people of Great Britain and America, and call upon God to create that hunger, be it by catastrophe, war, depression, or what not, that hunger, without which there can be no genuine Revival.

CHAPTER IX

IS EVANGELISM DEAD?

HAVE the glorious days of Evangelism passed and passed for ever? Will there never again be a Wesley, a Finney, a Moody? Are cities to be stirred no more by mighty revivals as in bygone days? Is it really true that the days of revivals are over, and that Evangelism is dead? My answer is "Yes" and "No".

The other day one of our Canadian papers came out with a picture of D. L. Moody and a brief account of his great Toronto campaign in Massey Hall in 1894. It told about the enormous crowds, about his preaching, and of how he publicly thanked Mr. Hart A. Massey, as he stood in his private box, for the gift of Massey Hall to the city. And then it spoke of Moody's great campaign as follows:

"The story of D. L. Moody is that of *a day of heroic Evangelism which has gone, perhaps never to return.* That epoch had a spiritual glamour of its own. There were no radios, no telephones, no trolleys, and not until Moody was a fairly old man, any electric lights."

In a later issue of the same paper, there was an account of the great meetings of the noted Canadian Evangelists, Crossley and Hunter, in Ottawa, when Sir John A. MacDonald, Canada's first Prime Minister, following a searching sermon by Mr. Hunter, rose to his feet and publicly professed his faith in Christ. That was in 1889, the year I was born.

A little while before he died, Dr. Crossley attended some of my services. Hunter, with whom for a quarter of a century he travelled in evangelistic work, had passed on. The present generation does not know him. To most of those now actively engaged in Christian service, the glories of the past have been forgotten. But, as I looked at Dr. Crossley, and other greyhaired warriors who used to be in the limelight of evangelism, I thought of the great scenes that were enacted more than a generation ago, when Evangelism was at its height, and I wondered if they would ever be witnessed by the

71

present or the next generation.

I have in my library an old shelf-worn volume of Moody's sermons, taken down in shorthand as he spoke. His ungrammatical sentences are recorded exactly as they fell from his lips. The instruction he gave from the platform, his warnings against hawkers, who were making gain by selling his picture, insignificant happenings - all are recorded just as they took place, and by one who was present and saw with his own eyes that of which he wrote.

I treasure that volume, treasure it because it is filled with the atmosphere of evangelism, an atmosphere with which the present generation is, for the most part, unfamiliar. For, as I read, I see again the great crowds, the thronging multitudes; I hear once more the soul-stirring sermons of the famous Evangelist, and I witness, as of yore, the scenes that meant so much to the Church a generation ago - days of Heaven on earth. But the question I am asking now is: Will they ever be repeated?

The heroic days of evangelism seemed to pass about the time I was in my teens. It was my privilege to get a glimpse of them in their fading glory at least. Well do I remember the great Torrey - Alexander meetings in Massey Hall, Toronto, in 1906, when I was converted. What impressed me was the large number of ministers of all denominations sitting on the platform. Then, too, my mind goes back to the spirit of evangelism in the Y.M.C.A. of a year or two later. Nor will I ever forget the meetings of Crossley and Hunter in Huntsville, Ontario, in 1908, and the impression they made on me. My young heart was thrilled whenever I came into contact with evangelistic services. But these were about the last. It was somewhere in the second decade of the twentieth century that the old-time spirit of evangelism took its flight.

GREAT CENTRES OF EVANGELISM

But - evangelism is not dead. By no means. Nor can it die, for it is God's one and only method of getting His work done. Hence, He is today raising up great nation-wide movements and centres specifically for evangelism, and in these the fires of evangelism will be kept burning.

These centres are established works, standing pre-eminently for the conversion of souls, the edification of believers, and worldwide evangelism, emphasizing especially the four essentials: Salvation, the Deeper Life, Foreign Missions, and our Lord's Return; endeavouring by every means to get the Message out to the Christless masses both at home and abroad in the shortest possible time.

The method followed is that of the Apostle Paul. He did not hold a brief campaign and pass on, valuable as that may be, but he remained in each place, if at all possible, until a real work had been established.

Every great city needs such a centre. Spurgeon, of London, took the Surrey Music Hall, seating 10,000, and the Crystal Palace, seating 20,000, and departing from all conventionalities, he preached the Gospel to the perishing multitudes of England's great metropolis, and then erected the Metropolitan Tabernacle, a permanent evangelistic centre.

D. L. Moody and R. A. Torrey had the same vision. They, too, believed, as Spurgeon did, in a centrally located work. Hence the great Moody Church, Chicago, the Church of the Open Door, Los Angeles, and The Peoples Church, Toronto, permanent centres of evangelism.

Some may be called to travel from place to place, but the most valuable kind of evangelism is done by establishing a headquarters where the revival fires never die out, and from that as a centre, working out to the entire world.

The generally accepted church idea - I mean a little group of believers meeting together on some obscure street, struggling to support a pastor, yet making no impression whatever on the multitudes - is surely not God's vision. How often do we find a mere handful of people overfed and underworked, self-satisfied and even anti-evangelistic, with no vision of enlargement and no sense of obligation to get the Message to the masses – a dried - up stagnant pool without an outlet. Only as our churches become spiritual centres for aggressive evangelism, both at home and abroad, will we be true to the vision of Jesus Christ as expressed in the great commission.

EVANGELISM SOLVES THE PROBLEMS

Evangelism will fill any church. It filled the Methodist churches, filled them all over the world for a hundred and fifty years. Methodism was born in evangelism: it lived and grew on evangelism. It has been the greatest of any evangelizing agency since the days of the Apostles. It got people saved and the converts filled the pews.

Moreover, evangelism will solve the financial problem. All Peter had to do was to catch the fish: the money was in its mouth. It is always so. Win the unsaved to Christ and they will supply the wherewithal to carry on His work. It is because evangelism has died that so many of our churches have had to be closed.

The Peoples Church has been no exception. All through the years we carried on a continuous ministry of evangelism and we still do. Evangelistic gospel songs are sung and soul-winning sermons preached.

Much use was made of the radio. For two and a half hours every Sunday night we were on the air, and thus multiplied thousands heard the Message and were evangelized.

Every Sunday night the invitation has been given. We do not merely preach and pronounce the benediction. We give men and women a chance to accept Christ by inviting them to the Inquiry Room. And it is doubtful if a week passes without souls being saved. Full well we know that the Church must either evangelize or fossilize; and so we evangelize, for the Church which ceases to be evangelistic will soon cease to be evangelical.

Our statement declares that we stand pre-eminently for the conversion of souls, the edification of believers and world-wide evangelism. There is nothing in that but what appears on the surface. We are old-fashioned, for we still believe in "the conversion of souls". Men need salvation. This neglected truth must be emphasized as never before. Then, too, believers are built up in the faith. And our evangelism is by no means confined to our own city. Thank God, it is worldwide. We believe and glory in the work of foreign missions.

THE FOUR GREAT ESSENTIALS

Now follow the four great essentials, viz.: "Salvation, the Deeper Life, Foreign Missions and our Lord's Return." Not that we disregard other important truths. By no means. But around these four, clusters most of the vital teaching of Scripture.

All that is meant by the Deeper Life we preach. God wants His children to be Spirit-filled and victorious over sin, to be a hundred per cent for Him; fully yielded, and entirely separated from the world and all its doings, that He may use them to the uttermost. We place the emphasis on Himself, a Person, rather than on gifts, experiences and manifestations. "Everything in Jesus and Jesus everything."

Then, too, the blessed truth of our Lord's Return we dare not neglect. That is the great hope of the Church. Our Lord is coming back. Detailed, personal interpretation of prophecy we do not stress. On that, men always have and always will differ. We can disagree and still be brethren, but we do insist on the all-important truth of our Lord's personal, visible return, and the establishment of His Kingdom.

Our statement closes with the words "endeavouring by every means to get the Gospel out to the Christless masses both at home and abroad in the shortest possible time". And, after all, that is the main thing. To live we must give. To take in we must give out. It was for this Christ came, lived, died and sent the Holy Ghost. This constitutes the supreme task of the Church. For this we exist. Our chief business is to get the Gospel out, to broadcast it by every legitimate means.

Especially are we to get it to the Christless masses. Unselfishly we are to be equally interested in getting it to the foreign as well as the home field, for by thus following our Lord's programme, which is to preach the Gospel "in all the world for a witness unto all nations" (Matt. 24:14), we can best hasten His return, since

God is now visiting the Gentiles in order "to take out of them a people for His name". (Acts 15:14)

Oh, what a vision! What a calling! What a work! How can anyone find fault with such a programme? Breathes there a man who loves the Lord and stands for the great fundamentals of the Faith, who could refuse to unite a hundred per cent in such a cause? How we should praise God for sound, sane, scriptural evangelism. A movement on fire for souls, born, not of man, nor of the will of the flesh, but of God.

Oh, then, let us evangelize, and let us keep at it, eternally at it, that men may have a chance to hear the Gospel and be saved. Let ministers, true ministers, give themselves to evangelism in their own pulpits, and make their local churches evangelistic centres, for God will bless evangelism as He will bless nothing else. He will set His seal of approval on it in the salvation of souls, the restoration of backsliders, and the edification of believers, for evangelism is still the order of the day.

> Go forth, go forth and win the lost,
> Evangelize whate' er the cost;
> The Gospel preach in ev'ry land,
> Go forth, it is the Lord's command.
>
> Evangelize in ev'ry tribe,
> The Gospel none must be denied;
> Go forth and tell of how He died,
> Go, tell of Christ the Crucified.
>
> Go forth and tell of how He rose
> And lives triumphant o'er His foes;
> Of how He's coming back again
> In pow'r and majesty to reign.
>
> He's coming back to take His Bride
> From ev'ry kindred, tongue and tribe;
> He's coming back to usher in
> The day of judgment for man's sin.
>
> Go forth, the message must be told,
> Go, bring them to the Saviour's fold;
> The Master calls. O then arise,
> Evangelize! Evangelize!
>
> O.J.S.

CHAPTER X

THE NEED OF THE HOUR

"WHERE there is no vision the people perish". (Proverbs 29:18) How true! Multitudes there are who throng our cities on every side, who are perishing simply because we have no vision. Christless masses for whom Jesus died may never hear God's message of salvation unless we get a vision. Our great centres of population for which we are responsible do not know the Gospel of God's grace because we, His followers, are without a vision. What are we going to do about it? When, oh when, will we get the burden and become conscious of our responsibility? True indeed is the verdict, "Where there is no vision, the people perish."

Snug in our little nest, comfortable amid our surroundings, satisfied with our handful of overfed followers, we hold our services, preach our sermons and seem to have no care, no thought, for the perishing multitudes around us. Yet God never told sinners to come to us. He told us to go to them. Why then do we blame them for not coming in when the real blame is ours for not going out? God help us. "Where there is no vision the people perish."

The world goes out into the open to attract attention. Theatres are built on the most prominent corners and brightly lighted, whereas the church, only too often, selects a back street, puts up a small building, installs dull lighting, and then wonders why the people do not attend. "The children of this world are wiser than the children of light." Every city needs a large, centrally located evangelistic work, brightly illuminated, easily accessible, capable of attracting the passerby, and with a real live, evangelistic programme, a programme geared to arouse the indifferent, awaken sinners and point them heavenward. Without such a vision, the people are bound to perish.

All that is needed to bring to pass such a God-given vision is faith, or should I say, faith and pains. Faith and pains will do anything. A God-given vision, a God-given faith, plus pains, namely; hard, sacrificial work, will accomplish the apparently impossible. Carey's motto sums it all up. "Expect great things from God; attempt great things for God." You cannot expect great things from God until you attempt great things for God. Get God's vision and then work it out. "All things are possible to him that believeth." "With God all things are possible." "Have faith in God."

We are living in days of awful apostasy. In my journeys through Europe, and more recently across Canada and the United States, I have been burdened regarding the religious situation and outlook as never before. The professing church, as prophesied, is fast becoming apostate. Many are turning from the Faith. This means that the entire world has now become one vast mission field. Thousands of regular churchgoers never hear the Gospel.

In many pulpits today, such statements as these are heard and that from ordained ministers of the Gospel: "I no longer preach the entire acceptance of the Bible. I do not preach the Heaven and Hell of the Bible and I do not know any worthwhile preachers who do. My education forbids my acceptance of the miracles of the Bible. I do not believe in the doctrine of salvation by blood. Thank God, I am not saved by the blood of anyone. Salvation by blood is the gospel of the butcher's shop." In view of such statements, is it not time that the true servants of God cried aloud and proclaimed once again the mighty soul-transforming truths of the old Book?

General Booth wrote "In Darkest England." God has been impressing upon my heart that terrible statement, "Behold, darkness shall cover the earth, and gross darkness the people". (Isaiah 60:2) This is true today, not only in the foreign field but here at home as well. People on every side are in almost total darkness, so far as God's salvation is concerned. Only here and there do we find a pulpit where the Gospel is preached, the new birth emphasized, salvation made plain and an invitation given. Altar services and inquiry rooms are seldom in evidence. Services are becoming more and more formal. In many churches the minister preaches as though everyone in his audience was already saved and bound for Heaven, yet in every congregation there are those who have never been born again.

Oh, for the preaching of Bunyan, Baxter, Aileen, Edwards, Wesley, Whitfield and Finney; preaching that made sinners tremble and cry aloud under a fearful burden of sin and guilt. May the Lord raise up such men again, men who, realizing the awful seriousness and responsibility of their calling, and laying aside all minor subjects, will fearlessly proclaim the great fundamentals of the Faith, that in these closing days of the age a clear and unmistakable testimony may be given. There is no other preaching, no other message, worth the time and effort.

Too much time is given to religious controversy. Why should we be on the defensive? Controversy has never been profitable. The truths of the Bible do not need to be defended; they only need to be proclaimed. The Bible will defend itself. It will survive long after its critics are dead and gone. We need a positive message. It was because of controversy in North Africa that the light went out, and it will happen here too, unless we change our methods.

Oh then, let us keep to our one great task of getting out the Gospel both at home and abroad. Let us work together in the unity of the Spirit. If we cannot agree on anything else, we can agree on evangelism. We all believe that the Gospel is the power of God unto salvation. Then let us preach it. Atheists have never been convinced by argument.

"No Attack! No Defense!" has always been my motto and it has stood me in good stead. I know of no better and I would strongly recommend that every minister make it his.

We are living, according to the Scripture, in the Laodicean days of the church. Therefore, the church itself must be evangelized. There must be a new call to separation from the world and whole-hearted devotion to Jesus Christ. How anyone who has been born again can remain in a church that is nothing more than a club, is beyond me. Compromise is always condemned in God's Word. The darkness must be dispelled. How else can we meet the fearful apostasy of the day.

The enemy is upon us. The storm is gathering and is about to break. Nothing but the preaching of the Gospel in the power of the Holy Spirit can stem the tide. Then let us evangelize. Let us go where the people are, and, with the best Gospel music, the best testimonies and the best messages, let us attract the Christless masses. Let us plan a bright, evangelistic programme and win them to our Saviour. Let us put Gospel booklets in every home in our community, and let us do it again and again.

Did you ever read Prov. 24:11,12? Searching words, these. Look at them if you will: "If thou forbear to deliver them that are drawn unto death, and those that are ready to be slain; if thou sayest, Behold, we knew it not; doth not He that pondereth the heart consider it? and He that keepeth thy soul, doth not He know it? and shall not He render to every man according to his works?"

What a striking statement! Who can read it and not be convicted? If men are threatened with death and we fail to warn them, we are to blame. We may plead ignorance. We may say that we did not know it. It will avail us nothing. We can know. We can find out the need. Such an excuse, God will not accept. We must sound the alarm. We must tell them of their danger.

This, my brethren, is the need of the hour. May God give us the vision, lest the people perish and we be held responsible.

CHAPTER XI

EVANGELISM! GOD'S ANSWER TO THIS GROANING WORLD

THIS is the twentieth century. Sinister forces are at work. False religions abound on every side. Nationalism is sweeping the earth. Communism, the most powerful weapon ever forged by satanic ingenuity, threatens to wipe out Christianity. Atomic energy holds civilization at its mercy.

I wish I could live to write the year 2000 A.D., but that can never be. Millions will, should Christ tarry; I cannot. I believe that the next fifty years will be the most momentous in the history of mankind. Events of world-shaking significance are already casting their shadows before them.

Colossal movements have been inaugurated; some for good, others for ill. The human race faces destruction. Cataclysmic judgments are inevitable. Revolution, with all its horrors, again lifts its hoary head. The Iron Curtain hides a slavery worse than death. All creation groans. The birth pangs of a new age are now being felt throughout the world. Once again there is "the sound of a going in the tops of the mulberry trees." "The coming of the Lord draweth nigh."

THE IMPORTANCE OF EVANGELISM

I am not a professional evangelist but I have carried on evangelistic work and I know that the only hope of our day is a new manifestation of the power of God. I have been in countries where I have seen that power in operation and I am confident that we can have here what I have witnessed there. *Evangelism is the order of the day, the need of the hour.* Without revival, life as we know it, must perish. We must evangelize or fossilize.

We all have our differences but there is one thing upon which we can unite, and that is evangelism. If we cannot get together on anything else, we should be able to work with each other in the winning of lost men and women to the Lord Jesus Christ. Ministers and laymen of all denominations should be able to co-operate when it comes to evangelism.

There are ministers who feel that they can do their own evangelistic work and that there is no need to import a professional evangelist. Let me say, and I base my assertion on forty years of ministry, for the most part as a pastor, that I owe the success of my work, in a large measure, to evangelism. The pastor of the church may be a good preacher, greatly beloved by his people, but even the best voice can become tiring. I have always welcomed others to my pulpit because I have realized that a new voice is imperative. An evangelist can win those I can never hope to win. Then when I take over again, my voice in turn becomes a new voice and thus the people never grow weary. As soon as I feel that they have heard me often enough, I bring in someone else to give them a change and the evangelist always leaves us with new friends, most of whom will stay with us after he has left.

The very first campaign I held in Toronto lasted for six months without the break of a night, Saturdays included, and generally two or three services on the Sundays. I managed the campaign and was the Chairman at all the meetings. But during the six months I had a dozen or more different evangelists, one after the other, to do the preaching. Thus I always had someone new to advertise and the people could continually look forward to a new voice. The crowds increased from week to week. Interest was intense and before it was over, many hundreds of souls had been saved, so that the work was greatly strengthened as a result. Every campaign more than paid for itself; for I saw to it that there was always something worthwhile in the treasury at the close.

All down the years, ever since, I have had two or three, and sometimes half a dozen campaigns each year, and in addition many special conferences of one kind and another. All of this has stimulated the spiritual life of the people, added new interest, created enthusiasm and consolidated the work. In between campaigns I have done the preaching and as the work became stronger and the crowds increased, I did more of the pulpit work myself, but I have never felt that I could do it alone. Even to this day I bring outside speakers to hold evangelistic campaigns.

THE DIFFICULTIES OF EVANGELISM

There was a day in the work of evangelism and revival, not so very long ago, when all the churches of a given town closed their doors and co-operated. It is no wonder that men like Billy Sunday got big crowds. For years Billy Sunday would not go to a town unless every church in the town agreed to close its doors and unite in the campaign. Consequently the choirs of all the churches were on the platform and more important still, the ministers. Since the churches were closed and the people had nowhere else to go, of course they came to the Tabernacle where the campaign was being held and filled it to capacity. Then, as they looked up and saw their own ministers sitting on the platform, they were inspired to co-operate, to give and to pray and to do whatever they could to make the campaign a success. That is the ideal way to win souls to Christ.

We are living in a day, however, when it seems next to impossible to get all the ministers of any one town and all the churches to co-operate. We are fortunate today if we can succeed in getting even the evangelical churches to close their doors and work with us, for even among fundamentalists there is so much division and strife that it is difficult to secure the necessary co-operation. But it is still true that *any town or city could be moved for God and a mighty revival could take place if the churches themselves would unite in a soul-winning effort and work together,* - ministers of all denominations, for the evangelization of the Christless masses on every side.

Sometimes it is objected that we need more Bible teaching, more Bible conferences, that we should give more attention to the study of the Word. Evangelism, it is stated, does not consolidate or teach. I beg to disagree. As I have studied the history of revival and evangelism all down the centuries, I have discovered that there is more teaching, more personal soul winning and that a greater number of people are inspired to study the Word of God during days of revival and evangelism than at any other time.

When the Holy Spirit is at work, the people naturally turn to the Bible and study it. Bible Classes are formed. Instruction is given in personal work. New converts testify and pray in public and as a result there is a greater knowledge of the Bible imparted than at any other time. *Bible teaching without evangelism will result in stagnation, but evangelism, which always produces Bible study, will inspire and bless.*

Then let me point out that it is the follow-up work that counts most, not the work that is done by the evangelist himself. The evangelist is like the doctor - he brings the baby into the world, but no one would ever expect the doctor to remain and take care of the child. That is the follow-up work which must be done by the parents. The doctor's responsibility ceases when the baby is born. It would be wrong to blame the doctor if the child did not develop properly after a healthy and normal birth, and it is just as wrong to blame the evangelist if the converts do not go on in the Faith and make progress after he has brought them into the light. That, I say, is the responsibility of others, namely, the pastor, the Sunday School teacher, the leaders of the Young People's work and all those who remain to take care of the new converts. If special converts' classes are organized, the converts can soon be established and taught the fundamental doctrines of the Faith so that they will stand true and steadfast and become active workers for the Lord Jesus Christ.

There is a lot of evangelism today that belittles the pastor. I am sorry to have to admit this, but it is true. *The kind of evangelism we need is that evangelism that will hold up the hands of the pastor and in every possible way support and encourage him.* For an evangelist to criticize or find fault in any way with a pastor before the people is a tragic mistake. He has enough to contend with in any case. He needs to be encouraged and the evangelist should do everything possible to make it easy for him. He should be honoured before his people. It is for this reason that I believe every evangelist, for a few years at least, should become a pastor so as to be able to sympathize with the pastor in his problems and know how to help him. He may not be perfect, but that may also be true of the evangelist and I am afraid that one of the reasons so many churches have turned against evangelism is because the evangelist has been discourteous to the pastor and has not given him the help he could.

Having been both a pastor and an evangelist, I know perfectly well that the work of the pastor is by far the most difficult and that the evangelist, in comparison, has an easy time. He only has to face the problems for two or three weeks in any one place, then he can leave. But the pastor is ever burdened with them. It is for this reason I slip away every now and again and hold a campaign, for it enables me to forget the petty problems of the pastor. Evangelists would do well to adopt a new attitude towards the pastors with whom they work.

THE NEED OF EVANGELISM

Do you know that the world evangelists are all dead? All except Dr. Billy Graham. D. L. Moody has gone; R. A. Torrey is no more; J. Wilbur Chapman has passed; Billy Sunday has finished his work and now my very dear and personal friend, the world-famous Gypsy Smith, has also gone on and, sad to say, there are very few on the horizon capable of filling the shoes of those whose names are household words throughout the world. That is because our seminaries and Bible colleges are not training evangelists. They are training pastors and missionaries but not evangelists. How many of them take up a study of the history of evangelism and revival? How many of them study the lives and methods of the great evangelists and revivalists of the past? How many of them teach their students how to conduct evangelistic campaigns?

There was a day when the great denominations of Canada, for instance, employed evangelists. Well do I remember when Crossley and Hunter, who worked together for a quarter of a century, toured the Dominion as the official evangelists of the Methodist Church of Canada. I remember because I was in their meetings. Today they are gone, and so far as I know none of the great denominations of Canada employ evangelists and yet our churches have been built on evangelism. Now other methods are being used, and as a result many pews are empty. Congregations have united and very few young people are being converted and brought into the church. What Canada needs today more than anything else, and what every denomination in Canada needs, is an army of evangelists or revivalists to go up and down the country, from church to church, and city to city, calling the people back to God.

I thank God for every evangelistic campaign, especially when all commercial aspects are absent. I know something of the harm that has been done because of the emphasis on finances, especially in connection with love offerings. I would like to see the day come when the evangelist, like the pastor, could be put on a definite salary from headquarters so that everyone would know exactly how much he receives and the accusation of profiteering and religious racketeering would never be heard. There should be a place in every denomination for the evangelist. He should receive a stated allowance from headquarters and all offerings over and above expenses should be turned in. That is perhaps the one and only solution to the problem.

We owe almost everything we have to evangelism. Most of those who have been converted have been converted in evangelistic campaigns or during periods of revival. I would say that sixty-two per cent at least have been reached for Christ through special meetings. Again and again I have asked for a show of hands and it has always been the same. What will happen, I wonder, when the Christians of today have passed on if there have been no campaigns in which to win others to Christ. In England the young people, for the most part, are gone. They have been lost to the church and the cry of the older Christians is, "Who will take our places when we are gone?" Evangelism is the only solution. Revival is imperative.

THE RESULTS OF EVANGELISM

As I have stated, I have majored on Missions and Evangelism down through the years. In the early days we had an average of approximately five hundred decisions each year. These newborn babes soon filled our pews with the result that the older Christians found their seats taken unless they came early. For years upon years we did no newspaper advertising whatever, so great were the crowds. I have had a letter from the Fire Chief demanding that I reduce my audiences because of the fire hazard. I read the letter to the people on a Sunday night when the church was packed with more than two thousand, many standing around the walls, others sitting on the steps in the aisles after numbers had been turned away, and the only result was that a still larger number tried to get in the following Sunday night.

We used to have a great pipe organ that occupied the entire space back of the gallery and when our people saw so many unsaved being turned away, week after week, in those early days, they began praying, asking God to send someone to buy the organ in order that a second gallery might be built in its place to accommodate more. After a few months God heard and answered and the organ is now in another large Church in Toronto. In its place we built a second gallery, above and back of the main gallery and the first night it was opened it was packed to capacity with scores sitting on the steps in the aisles and from that day to this, aside from the hot summer months, and the vacation season, it has been filled to capacity. Many scores, if not hundreds of souls, have come down from the elevation, as we call it, to get saved.

I have had the police walk in on me just before the service was to commence, insisting that I reduce the size of my audience, refusing to allow so many to stand around the sides or sit in the aisles. The only thing I could do, as I have stated, was to stop all newspaper advertising and even then, for a number of years, with scarcely an exception, I preached to more than two thousand people each Sunday night.

Evangelism will fill any church. I have proved it again and again and it will fill it week after week and year after year. Never will I forget the campaign that I was privileged to hold in the famous Park Street Church, Boston. Not only was it filled to capacity, but many were compelled to stand and at the end of the two weeks more than two hundred had made the great decision. The church was revolutionized. It has never been the same since.

God marvellously worked and what evangelism did for Park Street Church, it can do for any church.

The greatest campaigns of my life, until 1938, were held in Australia and New Zealand. Many times it was impossible to find places large enough to take care of the crowds. I ministered all by myself but from the very beginning God worked. The record has been published again and again. Extracts appear in my book *The Story of My Life*. Australia and New Zealand will never forget the campaigns of 1938. I had been stricken with malaria fever and yet, in spite of great weakness, God wrought. It was a miracle from beginning to end. At least one thousand found Christ and long before the campaigns closed the converts themselves had become my personal workers. It was a never-to-be-forgotten experience.

THE JOY OF EVANGELISM

After I had spoken to a large group of ministers in Sydney, Australia on evangelism I noticed a minister with a very sad expression on his face coming slowly towards me and I waited, wondering what was wrong. He stood for a moment before speaking and then, as I remember it, he spoke to me somewhat as follows: "Dr. Smith, do you really mean what you say?" "Why?" I replied, "What do you mean?" "Do you really mean," he emphasized, "that you believe it is possible to do as you have suggested?" "Well, what do you mean?" I asked again. "Do you think," he continued, "that it is possible for a Presbyterian minister to give an invitation?" and he emphasized the word "Presbyterian." "Well," I replied, "I am a Presbyterian minister and all during the days of my ministry I have extended an invitation and I have seen men and women in hundreds walk down the aisles to accept Jesus Christ as Saviour." "But you know," he answered, "it just isn't done. That isn't the way we do it in the Presbyterian Church." "I know it," I said, "but nevertheless I see no reason why even a Presbyterian minister should not give an invitation."

With a sorrowful expression he turned away and in a few moments I forgot all about him. The following Monday night, however, I was holding my meetings as usual in the General Assembly Hall of the Presbyterian Church and I was just about to ascend the pulpit steps when I noticed a commotion at the door. I paused, wondering what had happened. Presently, to my amazement, I saw the face of my friend, the Presbyterian minister of the past Saturday, struggling with a number of people at the door, and I realized that he was trying to force his way through the crowd, so I waited. At last he managed to get by and start rapidly down the aisle and I saw that he was making straight for me. Then, to my astonishment, I saw that he had a young woman on his left arm and another on his right and that he was tugging these two young women after him.

Finally he came within talking distance of me and I noticed that his face was illuminated and then I heard him call out, "It works, it works," and for the life of me I was unable to grasp his meaning. "What works?" I asked as he reached me. "Why," he exclaimed, "what you said Saturday. Sunday, for the first time in my life, I gave the invitation and look what I got" and with that he thrust the two young women in front of me. I questioned them and I discovered that they had both been soundly converted and then I remembered the incident of Saturday and it began to dawn on me that something had really happened.

He had given the invitation the day before but in fear and trembling. Two hands went up. He scarcely knew what to do but he asked those who had raised them to stand. The two young women stood to their feet. Uncertain what to do next, but remembering that I had invited those wishing to be saved to the Inquiry Room, he did the same. They came without a moment's hesitation. Not having any personal workers, however, he had to go into his vestry and deal with them himself, but he did so and they were saved. What a change. That Presbyterian minister went back to his work to do the thing he had neglected to do all his ministry. He went back to give the people to whom he preached an opportunity to accept Jesus Christ instead of pronouncing the benediction and going home. His whole ministry was revolutionized. He began to experience something of the joy of evangelism and he learned from experience that even a Presbyterian minister can give an invitation.

My suggestion to you, my friend, would be, "Go, and do thou likewise."

CHAPTER XII

EVANGELISM IN ACTION

CHARLES G. FINNEY is looked upon by authorities both in Great Britain and America as the greatest revivalist of all time. No man ever accomplished so much in so short a time. Not since the days of the Apostle Paul had such results been achieved. No one who values his reputation would ever dream of questioning the work of Charles G. Finney. Hence, in dealing with evangelism in action, we are going to turn first of all to the miraculous ministry of this great revivalist.

The first thing we must note in connection with the evangelism of Finney is that wherever Finney went, religion became the main topic of conversation. Every one was talking about the revival. All were interested in what was going on under the leadership of this man of God.

CAMPAIGNS TOO SHORT

Finney did not believe in short campaigns. Perhaps that is the reason we are not getting the results we should today. We do not give God a chance. Wherever Finney went, he stayed until something happened. He remained until revival broke out. Hence, his campaigns were frequently of great length. For instance, he stayed in the city of Philadelphia for a year and a half, carrying on his meetings night after night, preaching the Gospel of Jesus Christ, and labouring until revival broke out and the city was stirred by God.

Paul, you remember, followed the same method. He went to the city of Corinth and stayed there for a year and a half. Then he went to Ephesus and in Ephesus he spent three full years preaching, until the entire territory had been evangelized, until God had stirred the whole region and a mighty revival had swept all Asia.

When I commenced my work in Toronto, as previously stated, my first campaign lasted for six months. Week after week I brought evangelists to the city and carried on the meetings, day in and day out. The Gospel was proclaimed every night until six full months had gone by. Even Saturday was included. That was the foundation upon which we built the work. During those months God worked in a mighty way and the results have continued to this day. I had no trouble getting the choir to attend every night. The ushers and personal workers were in their places. The prayer warriors co-operated. Everyone was interested in the work.

I think one of the reasons why we do not have revival today is that our campaigns are too short. We do not give the Spirit of God time to work. There must be time for the sowing of the seed and then the harvesting of the crop. Sometimes conviction does not come easily and we are in too much of a hurry. We are anxious to see a harvest before the seed has been put in the ground, which, of course, is impossible.

AMAZING RESULTS

When Finney went to Rochester, he stayed until a revival actually broke out, until something happened, and I want to speak now about what did happen.

There was only one theatre in the city, and that theatre was closed and closed for good, as a result of the revival. The saloons were almost entirely deserted, so powerful was the revival. Crime was almost completely eliminated so that the courts had little to do. The prisons were emptied - think of what that would mean today, when our prisons are filled to capacity.

On the other hand, the churches were thronged and thronged to capacity. There was no need to spend money on expensive advertisements in order to make the services known. The churches automatically filled, filled until they were packed, and packed to capacity. And that went on for months and months. It became difficult for the people to find seats. You see, everyone was interested in the revival. Religion had become the main topic of conversation, not politics but religion. Not the weather or the international situation, but the revival. There was just the one topic of conversation. That is the way it should be today. So powerful should be the revival, that everyone should be talking about it. Moreover, all classes were reached. Not only the lower classes, but also the upper classes, the rich and the poor, children and adults, drunkards, the intelligentsia, scholars, leaders of society, lawyers and judges, bankers and doctors, skeptics and scoffers. There was not a class that was not influenced by the revival. Most of the leaders of society were affected, and many from among the highly educated were brought to the Lord Jesus Christ. Even scoffers were saved. God worked in a most remarkable way, so that every strata of society in the entire city was reached.

Restitution was made, debts were paid, obligations met. That always happens when there is genuine revival. I have seen it again and again. Those who have not been right with their fellow men have gotten right. They have squared with those they have wronged. In every revival there must be restitution, and there always will be restitution or else the revival is not genuine. Restitution is one of the natural results of the movement of the Spirit of God upon the community. One man, for instance, paid back thirty thousand dollars as a direct result of Finney's revival. That would be about one hundred and fifty thousand dollars today - and it was all paid within a period of six weeks. Revival brings apologies and reconciliations.

Another wonderful result was the recruiting of men for the ministry and the mission field. It was not necessary to beg young people to give their lives to God nor to appeal for volunteers for the regions beyond. As a direct result of the mighty awakening under Finney, there were young men on every side who entered the ministry and filled the vacant pulpits of the churches, as well as those who applied to go as missionaries to carry the message of God's salvation to those in darkness and midnight gloom. It is when there is no revival that it is difficult to get men to enter the ministry or to go to the mission field, but wherever the Spirit of God is at work, men are forthcoming.

CONVERTS WON

Converts were won. That always happens when there is real

93

revival. For instance, while Finney was holding his great campaign in the city of Philadelphia, a group of lumbermen happened to come to the city. These lumbermen were wonderfully and gloriously saved. They went back into the woods, and as a result of their testimony in the woods, no less than five thousand lumbermen were brought to the Lord Jesus Christ.

In one of Finney's meetings, as many as two thousand professed conversion. Have you ever heard of the like? What a miraculous work of grace. Think of it. Two thousand converts in a single service. Where today do such things happen?

On the day of Pentecost, there were three thousand added to the Church under the preaching of the Apostle Peter. Later, the number became five thousand. Finney had seen two thousand. Was it not another Pentecost? Now remember, these converts did not only sign cards, they did not merely raise their hands, they did not just come forward and stand at the front; they were definitely and gloriously saved. They had been born again, two thousand of them in a single meeting.

Finney at one time preached in an Anglican church and the Anglican rector of the church testified that fifteen hundred of his members had been soundly converted as a result of that one meeting. Think of fifteen hundred church members passing out of death and into life in a single service.

One day Finney went to a cotton factory somewhere in the States and preached just one sermon; but, as a result, almost every one in that factory was brought to the Lord Jesus Christ.

When Finney crossed the Atlantic to Great Britain, the results were the same. Everywhere he went there were great crowds, and on every side revival broke out, just as in the United States. Let me give you one example.

Finney was in London. He was preaching in Whitfield's Tabernacle. For several weeks he preached to Christians only, never once to the unsaved. Not a single invitation did he give. Week after week went by. Night after night, he proclaimed his message to those who had already professed conversion. Then, at long last, he turned to the pastor of the church and asked for an inquiry room. He said he wanted a room where personal workers could deal with souls.

The pastor offered him a room that would seat about forty people. Finney looked at him in amazement. He said, "Why, I want a room that will seat hundreds of people." Now it was the pastor's turn to be amazed. He was most skeptical, but to humour Finney, he gave him a hall, about a block away from the tabernacle, that seated fifteen hundred people, never dreaming of what was going to happen. Finney accepted it.

That night, when he gave the invitation - and it was the first time, remember, that he had given it - he asked all those who were anxious about their soul's salvation -no one else - to find their way to the auditorium a block away from the tabernacle, which was to be used as an inquiry room. When Finney reached the hall himself, he found it packed to capacity. There was not a vacant seat anywhere. People were standing on every side, and that night hundreds upon hundreds passed out of death and into life and were gloriously born again. From that day on, men and women throughout the British Isles came to Christ in multitudes, for revival broke out on every side.

Do you know that in one week, no less than fifty thousand people accepted Jesus Christ as a personal Saviour during the revival days of Charles G. Finney? Think of it, it you will, fifty thousand in only seven short days. That was a mighty movement of the Spirit of God, nor has it been duplicated since. When, I wonder, will we see it again? Oh, for such results today! It is said that within a period of ten years during the work of Finney in America, two hundred thousand passed out of death and into life. What a record!

There is nothing that we need more today than a mighty revival, a new manifestation of the Spirit of God. Those who feel their need the least, need it the most. Churches, colleges, Bible schools and seminaries that feel they can get along without a revival are the very ones that need a revival. Such results as I have mentioned cannot be obtained apart from revival.

ENROLLED IN CHURCHES

Not only were converts won; they were enrolled in the churches. Unless that happens, evangelism misses the mark altogether. Those who are brought to Jesus Christ should be put to work somewhere. They should do something definite for the Saviour.

Think of the results in Wales and America, of which I have already spoken. Do you know that within the short period of five weeks, no less than twenty thousand joined the churches of Wales? What miraculous results! What, I wonder, would happen in America if in any given city twenty thousand were to join the churches in a period of five weeks?

It is stated that when Charles G. Finney commenced his evangelistic work in the United States of America, there were only two hundred thousand church members in the entire country, but when he finished his work a few years later, there were three million names on the rolls of the various churches of the country.

Never in the history of the world had there been such results before. God used Finney to accomplish more than all the pastors of America put together during the same period.

Little do we realize how much we owe him. That, I say, is evangelism in action. That is the kind of evangelism for which we pray, the evangelism we long to see. When reporters come to me and ask the question, "What do you think is the great need of our day?", I always answer without a moment's hesitation, "A mighty manifestation of the power of God."

Dr. Henry Ward Beecher had this to say about Finney's revival work: "That was the greatest work of God and the greatest revival of religion that the world has ever seen in so short a time." That statement is of paramount importance. God grant that we may see it again. Oh, for another Finney!

POLAND

Have you ever seen revival? I have. It was on the Russian mission fields of Europe. But I want to tell you now of some of my experiences in Poland, Latvia, Australia and Jamaica. My entire ministry was revolutionized as a result. But let me describe them. I am quoting from my diary.

"In springless Polish wagons, we travelled through deep forests into the interior. Finally we arrived at our destination, and tears flowed freely as the converts surrounded us.

Two policemen with loaded rifles and fixed bayonets were present to watch and listen at every meeting. Long tables were placed in the open air, from which we were served with thick slices of black bread and raw herring, boiled eggs and wild honey. A countless number of flies swarmed over every thing. That night the women slept in the barn, and the men, side by side like sardines, on hay in the attic - about one hundred of us.

Sunday night a mighty wave of revival swept the audience, so that hundreds fell on their faces and wept before the Lord. Strong men sobbed aloud and with anguished faces gazed up, pleading with God to forgive and receive them.

Proceeding to another section of Poland, we found the church so packed that I had to be pushed through to the pulpit. At the close of my message, sobs were heard on every side, and soon a number had wept their way to Calvary. Later they testified with radiant faces to the joy that was now in their hearts. Some had travelled over two hundred miles in wagons to be present. I was told that at least five thousand souls had been saved during the previous five years.

With great difficulty we elbowed our way through the vast crowd. What a sight it was to gaze into the sea of faces on the ground floor and away up in the over-crowded gallery! Scores were standing in the aisles, nor was there any possibility of their sitting down for the next three hours at least. It was pouring rain outside.

How I wish I could describe the singing! As they joined in their great revival songs, I felt as though Heaven itself was bending low to listen, and I wondered if even the angelic hosts could more heartily praise and magnify the Lord.

At the close of my message I felt led to pray and, as I did so, it seemed as though a tidal wave of blessing broke upon the audience. First a single sob, then another, and yet another, until at last individual expressions were lost in the moaning and weeping that broke out all over the congregation. When I opened my eyes, I saw the faces of dozens, with tears flowing down their cheeks, broken and mellowed by the Spirit of God.

They needed no urging then, no coaxing. I only had to give a word of invitation and they responded in scores. There was no room at the altar, and even if there had been, it would have been impossible for them to move from where they were, so dense was the crowd. But they lifted their hands and gave every evidence of a wholehearted response. How many passed into the kingdom of Light I do not know. How many opened their hearts and received the Holy Spirit in His fullness, I cannot say. But I do know that God worked and worked in a mighty way. Glory be to His name!

The meetings at Luck were crowded out. The hall was by far too small. Not only were the aisles and side rooms packed, but many were unable to get in at all. When we saw the crowds we decided to rent the largest hall in the province, a splendid auditorium with two galleries, one away at the back above the first. But this too was crowded, aisles, doorways and all, and that in the morning.

A fifth of the audience were Jews. What an experience! Jews, listening eagerly to the message. People were amazed that they kept so quiet, but there were no interruptions of any kind. They fairly drank it in. Yes, the Jews will listen to the Gospel today, at least in Poland. Never will I forget their attentive faces as they stood or sat for three hours as though fascinated. At the last service on Monday morning some seventy-five responded to the invitation to accept Christ as a personal Saviour, how many Jews I know not.

And oh, how they sang my hymn 'Saved' in Russian. Again and again the glad proclamation was sung, 'Saved through Christ.' I doubt if the Jews will ever forget it.

Thus ended my work among the Russians in Poland, Poland so

soon to be devastated by war. What if I had been disobedient to the heavenly vision? How many who have since been executed would never have heard the Gospel?"

LATVIA

"Oh, what a sight greeted my eyes! Men and women were standing on every side, hundreds upon hundreds of them. The news had spread like wildfire. Finally, I preached and Pastor Fetler interpreted. For almost four hours the service continued. Scores knelt at the altar, weeping, praying and confessing their sins. More than three thousand were present and it was raining.

In amazement I gazed out over the vast audience. Not only were the pews full, but the great centre aisle was literally packed with people standing. Others were massed against the walls on each side, while many crouched on the edge of the platform. From high up in the gallery, great numbers gazed down. Never will I forget that scene. Oh, what a mission field! How ripened is the harvest, but where, oh where, are the reapers?

Next morning we held our service in one of the churches, where I spoke on the Holy Spirit. At the close, a woman came quickly to the front to ask forgiveness of two whom she had wronged. Scores knelt at the altar weeping and praying, utterly unconscious of those around. Sins were confessed and many bitter tears shed. My heart was deeply stirred as I listened to the plaintive tones of both men and women seeking God. The Spirit moved upon all hearts that morning, and for almost four hours the service continued with intense fervour.

Later I preached in the largest theatre and found it packed to capacity. What a sea of faces! I looked for aisles but could find none. People were standing in them from front to back. The gallery was crowded. Scores were compelled to stand throughout. What an opportunity! And, oh, the liberty, the joy! I concluded my message at nine, but Pastor Fetler went on with the meeting until 10.30. No one went home. There they stood drinking in every word.

When the invitation was finally given, some forty came and

knelt on the platform. A little girl, deeply convicted, cried aloud, saying she could not believe. A backslider came home. Finally all were dealt with, and with radiant faces returned to the audience. Still the huge congregation remained.

When we reached the great hall at night, we found it packed from end to end, the gallery full as well, and every aisle jammed. In spite of the cold winter night, they came. There was no fire in the building. I preached in my fur coat. Oh, how they listened! But how could we give the invitation; there was no room at the front. We dismissed the great audience and held an after-meeting. But not half of them left. The ground floor was still nearly full. Something else had to be done. So we cleared fifty seats at the front and gave the invitation. In a moment they were filled, and others who came had to stand. It was a glorious, never-to-be-forgotten scene. Men and women freely, gladly gave themselves to Christ. The meeting closed at 11.15 p.m.

We rented the largest halls available, but such crowds attended that great numbers were turned away. They jammed the aisles, sat on the window sills, stood on the platform, packed themselves into every corner, a huge, surging mass of men, women and children, ever moving, ever restless.

Oh, these multitudes! Will I ever forget them! What throngs of people! How great the harvest, but how few the reapers! What a mission field! They crowd our mission halls and are easily accessible.

Such is the virgin mission field I have now visited. My heart has been stirred, my soul burdened. With my own eyes, I have seen those teeming multitudes, and oh, how they have won me! Would to God I could spend months touring from place to place throughout Latgalia, telling the story to tens of thousands who have never yet heard. I received hundreds of letters of appreciation from the converts.

Now that I am back, I see again the surging throngs, the crowded aisles and the congested pews. I hear once more the plaintive songs and the fervent prayers of the people, and I feel anew the pressure of their hands as they plead with me to remain.

And as I remember their sad, tear-stained faces, I am conscious as never before of what the Master felt when He gazed with compassion on the perishing multitudes of old Judea long ago."

AUSTRALIA

"How shall I describe the service in the Lyceum Theatre? Talk about a crowd - they filled all the aisles, sat on the steps and stood everywhere they could, and then overflowed into the chapel where they listened through loud-speakers. But oh, what results! There were seventy-five who walked down the aisles to the inquiry rooms, each to be dealt with personally. The workers were swamped. What a break! There was deep, deep conviction.

Under the heading, 'There Was a Great Rain.' *The Methodist,* one of Australia's leading papers, published a report on the meeting and I am taking the liberty of quoting from it: 'The writer has attended many great religious gatherings of various kinds, but does not remember anything as wonderful as the evening service on Sunday last, when Dr. Oswald J. Smith of Canada preached the sermon. There has probably not been a greater crowd listening to any preacher in the Lyceum, in that the overflow for the first time was accommodated in Wesley Chapel, where amplifiers enabled the large company there to join in the service.

'Great expectation had been raised as reports of the Doctor's success in other services were circulated, and a keen spirit of expectancy was manifested by all present. A song session was conducted while the audience waited for the service to begin. Crowds stood throughout. When the appeal was made, in orthodox form, the response was immediate and almost overwhelming. Ushers were on duty directing the seekers to the four inquiry rooms - two for women and two for men. Each inquirer was personally dealt with, and the work went forward with mighty power. Tears were on most faces.' "

JAMAICA

"An eye-witness reports as follows. I quote him verbatim: 'When Dr. Smith gave the invitation on his opening Sunday night in Kingston, it seemed for a moment as though an avalanche had struck the theatre. Men, women and children streamed down the aisles to accept Christ. Like an army they came, some from the first gallery, many from the second, and scores from the ground floor. In a steady stream they mounted the steps, crossed the platform and entered the inquiry rooms. Each worker had to deal with a dozen seekers, there were so many. They needed no urging or coaxing. The movement was spontaneous. With serious faces and tear-dimmed eyes they flocked to the Saviour.

Some said they had never witnessed a break like it in Jamaica. The huge auditorium with its great balconies was packed to suffocation when the evangelist arrived. Even the large platform was crowded. Countless hundreds were turned away. All around the theatre and in the park near by, crowds stood, listening to the service and the message through loudspeakers. They were reverent and attentive. How many were saved or restored on that first Sunday night, only God knows.' "

This is a report of my second Jamaica campaign, held in the race-course grandstand, when my son, Paul, was with me:

" 'Dr. Oswald J. Smith has just held a great campaign in Jamaica, a campaign that almost became a revival. Night after night crowds gathered beginning with 4,000 and rapidly increasing until during the last week, according to the caretaker of the Race Course and many others, there were 10,000 present each night.

A conservative estimate for the last night would be 15,000. Most said 20,000. Over 475 decisions were counted that one night. The grandstand was jammed over an hour before the service commenced. Thousands stood throughout. Jamaica had seen nothing like it for any kind of meeting in its history.

It was a common thing to see 150 to 400 push through the great crowd night after night to accept Christ. The personal workers were swamped and had to deal with the seekers in groups. There were at least 2,000 who made the great decision, but there were many others whose names it was impossible to get.

The people packed every inch of sitting and standing space in the grandstand so that no aisles were visible. Then the vast open space in front which had been seated was likewise filled, thousands standing on either side. Hundreds of parked cars filled with listeners covered the field outside the fence, and scores upon scores who had climbed up, sat everywhere upon the roof. Never in all his ministry had Dr. Smith preached to such multitudes.

In order to deal with the converts the huge grandstand had first to be cleared while the seekers waited patiently at the front after having shaken hands with the evangelist, and then, surging up the steps, they were at last dealt with and led to Christ. In spite of the great crowd there was perfect order.

A conservative estimate would be an attendance of 150,000 during the two weeks of the campaign. They came in large trucks from various parts of the island. They were there at seven o'clock every night, and most of them an hour before. For two hours they stood in thousands shoulder to shoulder and scarcely moved. The newspaper compared it to the days of Wesley and Whitfield and said the Race Course had never seen the like before.' "

SOUTH AMERICA

"Buenos Aires was one of the eight cities in which Dr. Smith held campaigns in 1957. The auditorium accommodated 25,000 and as many as 5,000 were turned away on a single night. Some 300 churches co-operated. In the 8 campaigns, there were 4,500 first time decisions for Christ. Said Billy Graham: 'The Lord used Dr. Smith in South America to stir hearts as they have not been touched perhaps in the history of the Evangelical Movement.' These were the greatest campaigns of his life, greater even than South Africa, Australia, New Zealand, Ireland and the Scandinavian Countries."

What I saw on these fields, we must see here in the United States of America. Nothing else will solve the problems of the day, nothing but an old-fashioned revival. Again and again we should pray, "0 Lord, revive Thy work in the midst of the years, in the midst of the years make known; in wrath remember mercy". (Habakkuk 3:2)

I believe we are living in the closing days of this dispensation. Judgment awaits us, judgment or revival, mercy or wrath. If we will not have mercy, then we must accept judgment. Nothing but revival can save us. That is true of the individual. It is also true of the Church.

We are standing today at the cross roads. If God does not send revival, He may have to send judgment. It depends upon us as to whether it is to be judgment or revival. We can become ordinary ministers of the Gospel, or we can lay hold on the horns of the altar and give God no rest until He manifests Himself once again in mighty revival power.

CHAPTER XIII

LESSONS FROM EVANGELISM

THERE are six lessons that can be learned from the work of evangelism and revival. May God enable us to learn them until they become a part of our experience, for each one is of paramount importance.

1. LITTLE CAN BE ACCOMPLISHED APART FROM A MANIFESTATION OF THE SPIRIT OF GOD

That is the first lesson. Charles G. Finney, you will remember, was wonderfully converted. Directly after his conversion, he tells us, as he was standing before the fire in his office, he was baptized with the Holy Spirit. In his autobiography, he gives us a vivid description of that baptism. He did not speak in tongues, but something happened that made him the revivalist that he became.

The day following his conversion, you will remember, he went out into the village, and everyone to whom he spoke, even though he merely passed the time of day, was later convicted and saved, so mighty was the power of the Spirit upon him. That very night he sat down at the table and was requested to ask the blessing. As he did so, a Universalist who was present, stricken by conviction, rushed from the room, got down on his knees and prayed in agony before God until he was gloriously saved. And all because Finney had merely asked the blessing at the table.

When the Spirit of God comes upon a man as He came upon Finney, something unusual, something wonderful, something amazing happens. That, I say, is the first lesson we learn from evangelism and revival. Apart from the Spirit of God, little can be accomplished. Everything that Finney did was done in the power of the Holy Ghost. Everything that Evan Roberts and John Wesley accomplished was likewise accomplished as a result of a special manifestation of God's Spirit. Whatever was of abiding value was the work of the Holy Ghost.

2. UNFAVOURABLE CONDITIONS CAN ALWAYS
BE CHANGED BY THE POWER OF PREVAILING PRAYER

As you and I carry on our evangelistic work, we will often be confronted with unfavourable conditions. Things will not be just as we would like them to be. Everything, at times, will seem to go wrong, and nothing will be right. The people will not co-operate. There will be a lot of opposition. A strange spirit will characterize the meetings. The campaign will not be what you expected and you will reach a place where you will hardly know what to do. You may speak to this one or that one, and try to alter things, but you will find it impossible.

Now comes this second lesson which must be thoroughly learned, and every evangelist should be familiar with it. These unfavourable conditions can always be changed by the power of prevailing prayer. You and I must learn how to prevail with God in our evangelistic work.

Finney found that to be true. When things were not going right, he simply retired to the woods, where for hours he poured out his heart before God. Father Nash was with him to help him, not a song leader, but a prayer warrior. While Finney was preaching, Nash was praying. Every time Finney found himself facing a problem that he could not solve, he always went to prayer, for he had learned that any problem, no matter how difficult, could be solved by prayer.

When you and I learn, as Finney did, how to wrestle with God, how to travail in prayer, how to spend the midnight hours on our knees, we will then have learned the secret of victory over every difficulty. The early Methodists knew the secret. Again and again they would retire for prayer. They would spend hours wrestling with God, until, at last, they had prayed through and conditions were changed. You and I likewise will have to take hold of the horns of the altar and pray until the unfavourable conditions around us have been altered and prayer answered.

3. PERFECT OBEDIENCE TO THE WILL OF GOD
IS THE ONE PREREQUISITE TO SUCCESS

There is one thing in the life of Finney that arrests the attention. This is his implicit obedience to God. Even in the everyday details of life, Finney learned the will of God and then did it. We are told that he went to get the young woman who was to become his wife. On his way he stopped to have his horse shod, and while his horse was being shod, he was persuaded upon to preach the Gospel in the adjacent church. Soon, a crowd gathered; and as he preached, a revival broke out. The Spirit of God came down upon the audience. Men and women wept their way through to Calvary. Before long, the entire town was stirred.

Then the people endeavoured to persuade Finney to stay for another night and preach again. He did so, and the revival increased in power. After that he was persuaded to stay for a third night and again people got saved, conviction settled down upon the audience and the revival went on. So great did it become that Finney continued preaching, night after night. Finally, realizing that he could not continue his journey, he engaged another man to go for his bride, while he continued to preach the Gospel. That revival, we are told, continued for six long months. Finney never did get away, but he had been obedient to the Spirit of God. He had put first things first. He knew that he could get his bride later, but he realized that God's work could not wait.

How many, I wonder, would do that? How many would be willing to turn aside from their own plans and obey the Spirit of God? Could God find such men today, men who would be willing to break their own engagements in order to obey God? No wonder Finney experienced revival. He was sold out to God. God's work came first in his life. He was obedient at every point; hence, God used him for His glory and honour.

Perhaps God is telling someone now to turn from sin, to turn instantly from what he is doing. God expects obedience, instant obedience. What about it? Are we obeying? Are we doing the will of God? Do we turn away when God tells us to turn away? Do we do God's will when He reveals it to us? Are we living, moment by moment, in the centre of His Will? Or are we following our own inclinations? Do we refuse to listen to the Voice of the Spirit? No wonder God does not use us as He wants to. There must be instant obedience.

4. GREAT RESULTS CANNOT BE OBTAINED WITHOUT BOTH ENVY AND OPPOSITION

That is a hard lesson to learn, and yet, we will have to learn it. Many young evangelists start out thinking that there will never be any opposition, that everyone will welcome their ministry, and that they will be a success from the very beginning. They will not go far before they will realize that, if they are going to be successful, they will have to face both envy and opposition. There will be those who will be jealous of them, and there will be others who will oppose them.

Do not think that everyone will praise you, that other Christians will encourage you, that pastors will speak well of you and assist you in every way possible, and that you will have no difficulties to face. You might just as well know now, as you launch out into your life's work, that you are going to face envy and opposition. There will be many who will not co-operate with you. There will be those who will endeavour to discourage you, who will do everything possible to make your work difficult.

As long as you do not accomplish much, no one will bother much about you. But just as soon as you commence to become a success, just as soon as you are getting results, just as soon as people flock to your ministry, there will be those who will be envious of you. All you have to do is to accomplish something that no one else has accomplished, build something that no one else has built, get results that no one else has been getting, become a greater success than those around you, and the most deadly opposition will be yours. There will be jealousy and envy on every side.

Moreover, it will not come from the world. You would not be surprised if those who did not know Christ were to oppose you. But it will, in all probability, come from Christian leaders and

Christian workers, from those who ought to be standing by you and encouraging you in every way possible.

That is when you will feel like giving up. But if you know ahead of time that you must expect it, then you will be ready for it when it comes, and you will not be surprised. I say again, if God is going to use you in an extraordinary way, if He is going to do something through you that He has not done through others, you may be perfectly certain that you will be surrounded by envy and opposition on every side. That has been true all down through the centuries.

What about Finney? Was he ever criticized? Did he have to face envy and opposition? Do you know, the wonderful thing about it all is this, that as the years go by, the opposition, the criticism, the envy, the failures are for the most part forgotten. Seldom are they recorded. When you read the life story of a man, you only read the encouraging things about him, the successes, the victories. It is seldom that the other side is recorded. But let me say that Finney had about as much opposition to face as any man who has ever been used by God. And it was most diabolical. He was slandered on every side, and that by some of the most outstanding leaders of the Church of his day. For they were jealous of his success. Unitarian ministers fought him for years, so much so that he was always in the centre of a storm, in spite of the wonderful success he was having.

Dr. Lyman Beecher, one of the outstanding leaders of Finney's generation, did everything in his power to defeat him. As Finney approached Boston, Beecher sent him this message, and I quote it verbatim: "If you attempt to carry the fire to Boston, I will meet you at the state line and call out all the artillery men and fight every inch of the way to Boston, and then I will fight you there." Can you imagine anything more vicious than that? Well, then, what did Finney do? How did he answer him? What did he have to say? He never said a word. He made no reply whatever. He simply did what he always did. He went to the woods, to be alone with God. He began to wrestle in prayer. He told the Lord all about it, and God gave him a great victory.

That, my friend, is what you, too, should do. No matter what kind of a letter you receive, no matter how much opposition you have to face, just take it to God in prayer. Spread it before the Lord. God will fight your battles for you, if you will let Him. But, if you do your own fighting, God will let you do it, and then there may be defeat instead of victory. Learn how to pray. Never answer for yourself. "Vengeance is mine; I will repay, saith the Lord." Envy and opposition can both be overcome by prayer. God did it for Hezekiah. He, too, was opposed. He, too, received a letter, but he spread it before the Lord, and the Lord delivered him. So long as you know that you are in the centre of the will of God, you need not worry. Never mind the opposition. Pay no attention to the envy. Just go on serving the Lord. He will clear a way for you. God will gloriously vindicate in His own good time, and you will find that it pays to let Him fight your battles.

That is about the only kind of opposition and persecution that we get any more. We are not bound to stakes and burned alive. We do not have to suffer the death of a martyr. Seldom are we subjected to bodily injury. The only kind of opposition we get is criticism and slander, and that because of envy and jealousy.

For many years I have adopted a motto that has stood me in good stead. It consists of but four words: "No Attack, No Defense." I have passed it on to other evangelists, and they too have adopted it. They have learned that it works. I never attack anyone personally, and I never defend myself when I am attacked. I leave the matter entirely with God. God does not call you to attack others, and you do not have to defend yourself. He is able for every emergency. "As much as lieth in you, live peaceably with all men." If you will do that, God will bless you and use you and you will never need to fear the envy or opposition around you. "God is my defense." What a wonderful defense He is! Why not leave it in His hands? When you and I try to vindicate ourselves and fight our own battles, God has no alternative but to leave us to ourselves. But when we let Him defend us, then we are depending upon One who never fails. Hence my motto, "No Attack, No Defense."

Moody and Sankey had the same experience. When they went to Great Britain, they were opposed on every side. Newspapers ridiculed them and laughed at them. They even put in cartoons of them. Everywhere there was the most bitter opposition, and yet God so vindicated them that they won countless thousands to the Lord Jesus Christ in the British Isles. Today they are lauded and praised to the skies.

The Apostle Paul knew what it was to be opposed. Again and again he had an uproar on his hands. Everywhere he went he faced opposition, but God delivered him in spite of it all. You, too, will be delivered, but you will be opposed, and you must expect it. I warn you, therefore, lest you become discouraged. Expect both envy and opposition and these from Christian leaders.

5. PERENNIAL REVIVAL IS ONLY POSSIBLE WHERE THERE IS CONTINUOUS BROKENNESS OF HEART

Now we have found the secret. Do you want to have a heart always on fire for God? Do you want to know the continuous anointing of the Holy Spirit? Are you anxious to be used in the service of your Lord? Would you always be aflame with the power of God? Do you want a perennial revival in your own heart so that you will never lose your first love, your early enthusiasm? Are you praying that you may always be on fire for God and that you may ever be interested in the souls of men? Well, then, here is the secret. Perennial revival is only possible where there is continuous brokenness of heart.

Now let me ask you this question. How did Finney achieve perennial revival? Remember, to the very day of his death, he was a revivalist. He continually carried on soul-winning work. He never lost his burden for the lost. How, I ask, was he able to maintain such a ministry?

Every day of his life he made it a point to be alone with God and have a quiet time over the Word. Every day he made time for prayer. He never allowed a single day to pass by without meeting his Lord. That is the answer.

May I say that for over half a century now, I have observed the

Morning Watch. I would never dream of going to my work without first meeting God. Morning after morning I go to my study and wait upon my Lord. First of all I pore over the pages of the Sacred Book and then I give myself to prayer and supplication. Thus, I meet God before meeting men and He solves my problems before I come to them. The Morning Watch has meant everything in the world to me, and my ministry would be weak, powerless and ineffective without it.

Have you a time to meet God? Have you a place to meet God? Has there ever been a day in your life since you were converted when you have failed to open the pages of the Sacred Book and study the Word of God? Have you allowed a single day to go by without pouring out your heart in prayer and supplication?

My friend, if you want to maintain the spirituality that God has given you, if you want a perennial revival in your heart, you will have to learn to meet the Lord Jesus Christ from day to day. The manna, remember, was gathered daily. You, too, will have to gather it daily, or you will never amount to anything in the service of God.

There were times when Finney felt that he was getting cold, when he realized that his heart was becoming chilled. At every such time he resorted to extra hours of prayer. One time he spent a whole winter, never reading another book, never reading a newspaper, never reading anything else but the Bible, and that he read on his knees. Turning from everything else, he pored over the pages of the Sacred Book and gave himself to prayer in order that he might not lose the fire of revival. He wanted to keep a spirit of revival burning in his soul, and that is how he did it.

Again and again, he says, he received fresh baptisms of the Spirit of God, especially while he was spending time in prayer, or poring over the sacred pages of the Word. Time after time, the power of God came down upon him until his heart was warmed and set on fire once more. Then he went out to hold revival services and once again he saw conviction fall upon the people and hundreds upon hundreds were converted.

LESSONS FROM EVANGELISM

One of the greatest dangers of the ministry is to know the power of God in youth and then to lose it. There are so many who were once on fire, who were once interested in revival, but who have now lost the fire and have been set aside. It is easy to settle down in a comfortable parish, get a good income, enjoy all the luxuries of life, have everything run smoothly, and then lose your burden for souls. It is so easy for the passion for souls to leave you and to become mechanical. To be on fire when you are young, then to grow cold as the years come and go, is an experience that should never be yours. The only way to maintain the spirit of revival is to see to it that there is continuous brokenness of heart.

6. EVANGELISM IS THE SECRET OF MATERIAL
AS WELL AS SPIRITUAL BLESSING IN THE LOCAL CHURCH

The Alliance Tabernacle and The Peoples Church, Toronto, were both built on evangelism. Every campaign left money in the treasury. It did not all go for expenses or to the evangelist and his party; some was always left for the church. Thus the work prospered, materially as well as spiritually.

Unless there is financial blessing, there is mismanagement somewhere. The auditorium that costs the evangelist nothing to rent, with all its equipment, is surely entitled to some return. Otherwise it is not worth the investment. The pastor who labours to train workers, and who without any extra remuneration, toils and plans for the campaign, should surely see to it that the campaign leaves the church better off financially as well as spiritually.

God's will is clearly set forth regarding material blessings. "Beloved, I wish above all things that thou mayest prosper and be in health, even as thy soul prospereth" (3 John 2.). The three, you see, go together, spiritual, physical and material prosperity. There are exceptions but that is God's highest will. If the campaign is a spiritual blessing to the church, it will also be a financial blessing. The two cannot be divorced.

These, then, are the six lessons that can be learned from evangelism and revival. Each one, as I have already stated, is of paramount importance. Unless you and I thoroughly learn them, we will not profit much by what we have read and seen of revival work. May I say again, therefore, that little can be accomplished apart from a manifestation of the Spirit of God, that unfavourable conditions can always be changed by the power of prevailing prayer, that perfect obedience to the will of God is the one prerequisite to success, that great results cannot be obtained without both envy and opposition, that perennial revival is only possible where there is continuous brokenness of heart, and finally, that evangelism is the secret of material as well as spiritual blessing in the local church.

"If my people, which are called by my name, shall humble themselves, and pray, and seek my face, and turn from their wicked ways; then will I hear from heaven, and will forgive their sin, and will heal their land." (2 Chron. 7:14)

CHAPTER XIV

HEART YEARNINGS FOR REVIVAL

PERHAPS the best way to tell the story of what God did when I was in charge of Dale Presbyterian Church, will be to quote from my diary. Space forbids a full account. It is only possible to select portions here and there; but these, I believe, will be sufficient to stir up a spirit of Revival and thus glorify the Lord. I was now 27 years of age.

TORONTO, AUGUST 16TH, 1917

It must come, the Revival for which I have prayed so long. How God melted me this morning! How sweet is prayer! Praise His name! Oh, for Holy Spirit conviction and Holy Spirit fruit! Only that will stand the test of time and Eternity. God has stirred my heart in an unusual way. How unspeakably precious He is. Oh, for conviction, old-fashioned conviction of sin!

Thanks be to God for these wonderful books! How they have helped me! My preaching has been revolutionized. Have been reading them hour after hour. Never got hold of anything like them in my life before: "An Alarm to Unconverted Sinners," by Joseph Alleine; "The Anxious Inquirer After Salvation," by John Angell James; and "A Call to the Unconverted," by Richard Baxter. These are the books. How clear and definite their message on Sin, Salvation, Heaven and Hell! Yet I realize that even these truths may be proclaimed without results unless there is the power of the Spirit. He must convict. "Not by might, nor by power, but by My Spirit, saith the Lord of hosts," And this is, perhaps, the secret of failure. Truth is preached most earnestly and faithfully but nothing happens. What is the matter? No power.

During my intercession this morning I read a few chapters from "Memoirs of John Smith," by Richard Treffry, and it drove me to prayer. For some time God gave wonderful liberty, perhaps an hour, possibly less. I don't know for I was entirely unconscious of time. And first He led me to confession. Oh, how I have failed!

Failed in prayer, for I have spent minutes when I ought to have spent hours. Failed in Bible study, for I have not pored over the sacred pages as I ought. Failed in time, for I have allowed Satan to fill my life with other things and thus crowd God out. Failed in service, for I have not given out gospel tracts to the unsaved, nor spoken to them personally about their soul's salvation. Oh, I have failed, miserably failed. And I long to be true and faithful. I plead for souls, yet my eyes do not weep as His did.

But, glory be to God, I believe He is leading me into a deeper experience where I will count all things but loss for Christ; where I will suffer, sacrifice, pray, study and serve as never before; where there will be but one thing in my life, and thus the Revival for which I long will come. He will pour forth His Spirit, souls will be convicted and saved. May God hear and graciously answer! I must not fail again. God help me to press on, and on, and on.

AUGUST 25TH

In my reading this morning my attention was specially drawn to the following verse: "Herod feared John, knowing that he was a righteous and holy man" (Mark 6: 20). Oh, the power of a holy life! Wicked men fear and tremble in the presence of holiness. May God make this an incentive to me. I am reading the New Testament through rapidly for the purpose of selecting those truths which will bring conviction when preached in Holy Spirit power. God is giving searching messages on Sin, Salvation, Heaven and Hell. Spent an hour in prayer with Samuel Stevenson and had sweet fellowship. I want to know and experience more. Never will I be satisfied until God works in convicting power and men and women weep their way to the Cross.

AUGUST 26TH

His message to me this morning was, "All things are possible to him that believeth," and, "This kind can come out by nothing save by prayer". (Mark 9:23,29) Prayer and faith are both necessary for results: Thus the power of Satan will be broken in the hearts of men, and Holy Spirit fruit produced. "Lord, I believe;

help Thou mine unbelief."

Gathered three into my study this evening. Expected others but they did not come. Talked to them for about an hour. Found much sympathy and willingness to co-operate, but almost entire ignorance as to Holy Spirit fruit and the outpouring of God's Spirit. Decided to meet again along with others to talk it over that we may pray intelligently. Came home rejoicing, for I firmly believe that God will move upon the hearts of the people in answer to prevailing prayer.

AUGUST 31ST

Eight gathered in the church study to-night, and we talked and prayed until after ten. Much prayer had been offered that His Spirit might open their eyes and let them see the need and feel the responsibility. If God has chosen them, they will stand with me; if not, I will have to go on alone. We have decided to hold cottage prayer meetings, one each week to begin with. In closing, I gave them this verse over which we prayed: "If my people, which are called by my name, shall humble themselves, and pray, and seek my face, and turn from their wicked ways; then will I hear from heaven, and will forgive their sin, and will heal their land". (2 Chron. 7:14) Samuel Stevenson was one of us.

SEPTEMBER 2ND

Preached to-night. Had liberty and a little power. People at great tension. Searched the faces in vain for signs of soul anguish and distress. Eyes dry. No outward token of conviction. Surely I am not yet endued with power from on high. If so, there would be Holy Spirit fruit.

SEPTEMBER 7TH

"We have toiled all the night and have taken nothing". (Luke 5:1-11) But when they let down their nets under Divine leadership "they enclosed a great multitude of fishes." Has this been my experience, or do I labour in the flesh instead of in the Spirit? Truly, I "have toiled all the night and taken nothing." If men do not tremble and go away distressed and broken it is my fault. I

117

THE PASSION FOR SOULS

must take the blame. When I agonize and travail over souls there will be results, but not before. Then to my knees and on my face until the power comes and God can manifest Himself. Prayed nearly all afternoon, but not much freedom. Heavens like brass.

SEPTEMBER 9TH

"But we will give ourselves continually to prayer and to the ministry of the Word". (Acts 6:4) Once again it must be that I have preached in the flesh and not in the Spirit. Had much liberty and power and felt that there was considerable conviction. The people listened most attentively and there was a great deal of discussion afterwards. Yet nothing happened. No one broken. No distress manifested; no soul anguish; no tears. Oh, for God's power! (Luke 24:49; Acts 1:8; Zech. 4:6; John 6:63).

He has chosen me that I should bring forth fruit, fruit that will remain and stand the test of time and Eternity (John 15:16). Yet I am not doing it. There is but little fruit. However, it sends me to my knees. There must still be hours of waiting upon God. The price has to be paid. And when the Spirit comes upon me and fills me I will know it by the evidence of Holy Spirit fruit. Short of this I dare not rest.

SEPTEMBER 11TH

Glory be to God! There has been a move at last. It occurred in the cottage prayer meeting to-night. The service at first was cold and the people unresponsive. I spoke on prevailing prayer, concluded and closed. But no sooner was the meeting over than a woman suddenly cried out: "Pray for me, a church member" - and the rest was drowned in a flood of tears, great mighty sobs that shook her whole body. There was no let up, nor could we speak. She sobbed and sobbed as though her heart would break. Down we went on our knees and prayed one after another. Then we sang, "Just As I Am," and in about fifteen or twenty minutes she came through gloriously saved. Blessed be the Name of the Lord!

Oh, how our hearts thrilled with joy. Scarcely could we speak. All the way home I could hardly contain myself. Only two meetings and God had come. Prayer was answered. The Holy Spirit had commenced to work, for one soul, at least, had been broken up. A church member – unsaved! I wonder how many others are in a like condition?

SEPTEMBER 12TH

God is surely working. Another young woman, who had been convicted, got up to-night and testified that she was saved yesterday at her work and received full assurance this morning. Praise God! He has again answered prayer. She says she has done almost nothing else but pray all week. So now we have two brought in through the power of God alone. It is for this I have been burdened, the coming of the Holy Spirit in such mighty convicting power that souls would cry out for mercy without even an invitation. God has set to His seal and honoured His truth.

SEPTEMBER 16TH

Spoke to-night and had unusual liberty and power. People listened intently. Many eyes were filled with tears, but there was no break. However, I am convinced that God is preparing His servants and that He will yet manifest His power in the conversion of others. It only means that I must spend many more hours in prayer this week than last.

SEPTEMBER 18TH

Powerful cottage prayer meeting. House full, prayer fervent. Many hungry for God. Meeting continued until nearly ten o'clock, yet no visible sign. I must experience God's power no matter what it costs. Oh, that He would break me down and cause me to weep for the salvation of souls!

SEPTEMBER 19TH

Another break to-night. A backslider tried to pray in the meeting but immediately broke down and wept out her confession. She continued to pray in broken syllables, weeping at the same time. Thank God for this, but oh, for an intensified effect! Am still far from satisfied.

Another who has had a terrible struggle asked me to-night if she must confess having stolen something. So God is working.

SEPTEMBER 21ST

Received a letter this morning from one in great distress and went to see her at once. Found her weeping in anguish of spirit. After prayer God wonderfully met her and it was good to see the glow of joy in her eyes when leaving. God is surely working with her. Praise His name! More and more I feel the need of prayer.

SEPTEMBER 22ND

Have just finished reading "Glimpses of Life in Soul Winning," by James Caughey. Oh, what passion, what devotion and whole-hearted earnestness, and what a record of souls saved! Months of battling in prayer, then the victory. I do not believe that there is power enough on earth or in hell to prevent a revival if I am willing to pay the price.

SEPTEMBER 24TH

Went to-day to the home of my friend, Dr. E. Ralph Hooper, the beloved physician, and had a couple of hours with him in prayer. Was greatly discouraged over last night's service. No liberty, no power, no freedom to preach. Everything was hard. Feel I am just playing with prayer. Must spend more time in intercession. Mr. Stevenson was also present.

SEPTEMBER 25TH

Three of us met this morning and prayed for four hours. Experienced much blessing. Yet at the cottage prayer meeting to-night there did not seem to be a move of any kind. Two or three confessed sin, while one young man broke out and prayed.

Have been greatly impressed with Joel 2:18 and 28-29. There it is, the need, the methods, and then the results. But I can't do it myself. My heart is cold and hard. I do not weep and mourn. May God melt and break me and then work mightily among the people. I found Jer. 5:14 also a great and precious promise and have prayed it on my knees: "I will make my Words in thy mouth fire,

120

and this people wood and it shall devour them." God grant that it may be so.

SEPTEMBER 26TH

Glorious break to-night. The prayer meeting seemed cold and dead. Very few prayed. I spoke and closed the meeting, disappointed. Then a woman started to weep. She was followed by another, and later on a third was broken by God's power. All gathered around and prayed. The first two sobbed and sobbed as though their hearts would break, praying and confessing by turns. Oh, it was glorious. God was working mightily. One of them who had stubbornly refused to pray in public the first night and who had sat throughout the meeting utterly unmoved, now wept so bitterly that she was unable to speak. Finally all went home fully satisfied, the light of Heaven in their faces.

I saw that a fourth was under conviction as the result of what had just taken place. She is one of our prominent members. I simply shook hands with her, feeling that it would be best to leave her alone and let the Holy Spirit do His own work. As she passed out there was a look of anguish on her face and her handshake told the story. How wonderfully God uses conversions to bring conviction upon others. Can it be that the Revival has started?

OCTOBER 3RD

Once again I have cause to glory in God. He has given another sign of His presence and power. One other has been convicted and saved and is to-day rejoicing in God. Six weeks I think it has taken. Now she is free. God has brought her into clear and abiding liberty. In the meeting to-night she testified, her one-time dejected face shining with the light of Heaven as she told how she had found the peace which passes understanding, saying it was worth all the struggle. Praise God! I believe the work is genuine.

OCTOBER 4TH

Spent this afternoon in prayer with Samuel Stevenson. Then went to Dr. Hooper's home for the evening where we continued in prayer until a quarter to twelve. Oh, for the power of God!

We have it. How wonderfully He opened His Word to us while in prayer. We have read it and prayed it on our knees, especially the second chapter of Joel. Oh, for a baptism of tears! Also the ninth chapter of Daniel. Sentence by sentence we prayed it out before the Lord. We are surrounded by mountains of unbelief and opposition on every side. Only the power of God can overthrow them. "Have faith in God." I want to be wholly absorbed in Him. One passion - Christ.

Lately I have been reading Robert Murray McCheyne, George Fox, Billy Bray, Chas. G. Finney, Henry Moorhouse, John Fletcher, George Whitefield, David Stoner, Henry Martyn, John Wesley, John Bunyan, Thos. Collins, James Caughey, John Smith, David Brainerd; and oh, what men of God they were! What examples of devotion, zeal and piety! Would I could be like them! What a wonder was Wm. Bramwell! But where am I? Oh, to burn out for God! All, all for Him. Jesus only. Souls! Souls! Souls! I am determined to be a winner of souls. God help me.

OCTOBER 5TH

Once again, thanks be to God, there has been another conversion. This time a man. He came into my study to-night and told me that he had been convicted in a previous meeting and was most miserable. He had made resolutions again and again and had even tried religion but was still unsaved although he was a member of the church. Yesterday he threw his pipe away. I prayed with him and then we went into the service. Near the close of the meeting he stood up and confessed to all what he had already related to me. His eyes were filled with tears. Yet in spite of this he did not get through. I came home and settled down to pray for him most definitely, pleading with God to let him see the light and enable him to believe.

Faith is rising to assurance. God is working. Deep conviction has already settled upon many. Oh, for a mighty break! Have found Mark 11:22-24; Joel 1:13,14,16; 2:1, 11-18, 25, 28, 29, most precious to-day. Have prayed them one by one before God.

OCTOBER 8TH

Very strong opposition. Some of the leading officials object publicly to the meetings. Worldly members up in arms. Satan is beginning to give evidence that he is also interested in what is going on. Have taken it to the Lord in prayer. Continued intercession this evening from about eight o'clock until a quarter to one in the morning with Dr. Hooper and Samuel Stevenson.

OCTOBER 10TH

Dr. Hooper, Samuel Stevenson, the Man of Prayer, and I spent the day waiting on God, and, as a result, we had a good meeting to-night. Many testified splendidly for over half an hour. Indeed, I had to restrain them in order to give time for prayer. God is working, conviction deepening and spreading. Lives are being changed, souls coming into abundant joy and glorious liberty.

OCTOBER 11TH

God's Word is becoming so precious. We are hearing His voice through the prophets of the Old Testament. Our method is to read a little and then pray it out before God, closing by asking Him to fulfill it in our experience.

"That which is born of the flesh is flesh and that which is born of the Spirit is spirit" (John 3:6). If we work in the flesh our fruit will correspond and souls be brought into a false experience. Lord, give us Holy Spirit fruit. We have taken the method of prayer as commanded in God's Word. Every other method has been tried and is being tried to-day, but the results do not satisfy. So now if we do not prevail in prayer we will become a reproach and to that extent prayer will be discredited. We cannot afford to fail. We must give ourselves continually to prayer and the ministry of the Word. If our lives do not convict people of sin there is something wrong. Oh, for the faith of the Syro-Phoenician woman! She would not take "No" for an answer (Mark 7:24-30).

OCTOBER 14TH

Preached morning and evening with freedom and liberty, but no apparent result. Am still unsatisfied. Yet God is working a little. A man has restored stolen money to his employer and a woman has given back funds that were taken from the Sunday School as a result of the convicting power of the Spirit. But I pray for the conviction to spread and deepen. Oh, for souls to be wounded! Have been reading the diary of David Brainerd. Months and months of agonizing prayer, and then the mighty power of God upon the Indians. I must have Holy Spirit fruit, nothing less.

SPIRITUAL EXPERIENCES

AUGUST 26TH

Last week I wrote to George W. Stenton, of Peterborough, insisting that he come to help me in prayer. He came and we have had a wonderful time together. This afternoon when I announced that supper was ready, he lifted his head from the floor with a look of amazement on his face. His eyes were filled with tears. He looked as though he had been in Heaven and had been suddenly hurled to earth again, for he was all melted and broken up. God has given him a great faith and he knows how to hold on in prayer. The answers he receives are amazing. It inspires faith in others for he lives with God.

SEPTEMBER 9TH

The Word is becoming more precious to me all the time. I delight in reading chapters from the old prophets. My heart hungers for a fuller experience of God's salvation and a closer walk with Jesus Christ. I want to be weaned from the world and all it contains. The more I pray the more I love to pray. God is my portion.

SEPTEMBER 15TH

God has tonight set His seal, borne witness to the truth, and confirmed His Word. While I was preaching, a young woman, who was a stranger, rose to her feet and stood still for some time before I observed her. I stopped speaking, praised God, and asked her if she had decided for Christ. From her answer it appeared that she could not wait until the close of the service, so deeply had she been convicted. Then I went on with my sermon. The effect was wonderful. An awe overspread the entire congregation and scores were deeply stirred. As I went on three men and two women were observed weeping. One man sobbed aloud. The young woman who had stood came to my study after the service, and, so far as I could tell, was clear in her pardon. How we praised God!

SEPTEMBER 23RD

There must be more soul-anguish and deeper conviction of sin, but this is wholly the operation of the Spirit. Therefore nothing but the prayer of faith will avail. It is God who saves souls. The work of God is the operation of the Holy Spirit in answer to the Prayer of Faith. I have read the life of John Smith once again. What a man of prayer and faith he was! And how he aimed for souls! There are many books that describe revival and relate the results of God's work, but John Smith tells me how to get it, how to do it, the method, the only method that produces Holy Spirit fruit and procures an outcome for God's glory.

Am now reading the Journals of John Wesley for the first time. Four large volumes. Will I ever finish them! I think so, for I find them intensely interesting and helpful. Oh, what a man he was! And how wonderfully he proclaimed the great fundamental doctrine of salvation by faith alone.

Miss Alice Porter, my deaconess, Mrs. Charman, Mrs. Scott, Mr. Weir, Mr. Hutchinson, Dr. E. Ralph Hooper, and. Mr. Samuel Stevenson, the Man of Prayer, who introduced me to most of the books I have mentioned, and my wife have been my main prayer-warriors.

Work on, Thou Spirit of Power, and raise up once more a people for Thy name! Grant us again a visitation from on High, a return of revival days, for surely this is Heaven below! And in it all may Jesus Christ be glorified. Amen!

"He who would preach powerfully
must pray effectively" - O.J.S.